Living in the New Creation

Reframing Your Life

REV. MICHAEL LESSARD

Copyright © 2022 by Rev. Michael Lessard.

ISBN 978-1-64133-888-2 (softcover)
ISBN 978-1-64133-889-9 (ebook)

All rights reserved. No part of this book may be reproduced or transmitted in any form or by any means, electronic or mechanical, including photocopying, recording, or by any information storage and retrieval system without express written permission from the author, except in the case of brief quotations embodied in critical reviews and certain other noncommercial uses permitted by copyright law.

Printed in the United States of America.

Brilliant Books Literary
137 Forest Park Lane Thomasville
North Carolina 27360 USA

Preface

In my first book of this series, *Christology of the Family*, I wrote about the importance of the sacramental nature of the family. I also described the model of a pastoral care church (community). The novel *The Lost Dutchman* is a story that brings to life the themes of *Christology of the Family*.

In volume 2, I want to move us forward to consider the implications of this model in Christian moral theology and the necessary conflict with specific elements of our modern culture. The foundation of our present cultural moral climate has a lot in common with similar fundamental questions that also burdened our ancestors: why do we suffer, and what does it mean? Certainly science and technology have come a long way, and we have many new tools in medicine to deal with suffering. However, the other side of that truth is the fact that for many with serious health issues, the suffering lasts longer, and pain becomes a chronic way of life. Part of our fear is not about what medicine can do for us but what it can do to us. Yes, we can, for example, perform bypass surgery on an eighty-year-old patient, and he or she might survive the procedure, but he or she may live the rest of his or her life on a ventilator because of complications like a stroke, pulmonary issues, or infections. I have seen, as a hospital chaplain, wonderful medical interventions that make the blind see and the lame walk and those near death brought back to life. I have also witnessed the futility of surgeries that have failed. Often these failures attack the soul and body of the patient with repeated questionable procedures that only caused more complications. When the medical model fails, often it's the patient who gets blamed. There is *an ethical* question: if we can do some medical intervention, does it necessarily mean we should do that procedure (Degrazia, et al., 2011)? We will start together on this journey, describing the problem of "belief" in our modern culture, and we will look at how Jesus and the early church responded to the clash of worldviews between paganism and Christianity. We will draw from that reflection the similarities today in our American culture and set a course in this book that leads to the heart of the Gospel's invitation to love and care for each other in Christ, His new creation, its principles, and their application into moral and ethical decision-making.

Living in the New Creation

1 We stand upon what came before
the regiments of generations.
The forward march of human corp—
the reveille of nations.

*

2 The army that guards the post,
carries its banners on display.
Charging with enterprise, rank, and class,
wrapping their colors around today.

*

3 Oh, the colossal carnage of daily battle,
the roar of conflict upon the earth.
Drumbeats of sorrow, death's saber rattles—
the noise of strife signals our curse.

*

4 We stand and wait for Him to come again.
When the trumpet will sound taps,
and all the wars and hate will end,
and we will bivouac in God's camp.

*

5 Till that day arrives, we balance the time,
and center our optics on that future day,
ambivalent, half there or left behind,
still vainly trying to brush the past away.

*

⁶ We find no perfect place, no garden unbowed.
No pleasure without another expectation,
setting the bar high-wired and proud,
yet wondering in the tumbleweeds of limitations.

*

⁷ Praise God for the gift of our emancipation!
The fertile soil of Christ's Harvest of Redemption,
pregnant with the glorious gift of His salvation.
Not alone with feigned regret, "Now the new creation!"

*

⁸ I look into the pool of love's tranquil oasis—
reflecting the image that God has presented,
with light, and shimmering incandescence,
illuminating the Adam His Spirit resurrected.

*

⁹ I hear the gurgling, bubbling, sloshing sounds,
of water, rivulets, birthing an ocean of crescendos.
A tidal force that crashes, retreats, and rebounds,
with ancient percussions, vibrations, and echoes.

*

¹⁰ I feel a stinging tiredness that time is almost over.
It's a challenge to gulp down air yet grasp the prize.
Arms locked across my chest, clutching life's preserver
kicking and straining, hard against the tide.

*

¹¹ Amid this fugue, a tiny voice breaks through.
The sound is hard to hear, yet so familiar.
The faint and distant symphony of tender things I knew,
a memory of bliss, a will of the wisp, a whisper.

*

[12] "Step into my Father's moonlit valley," it says.
"Walk down the path and smell the perfumed air.
Come closer, in the hollow of creosote and sage,
the tingling garden of creation. Wait for me there."

*

[13] Carefully, I went unsure, unsteady with each stride.
I glanced side to side and focused my eyes all around.
The cool evening fog secured me with its misty tie,
not afraid of what I'd find, only hoping that I'd be found.

*

[14] I came upon my friend's silhouette, light against the dark.
Closer, ever closer, I approached…reaching out my arms.
I saw the love in your smile that lit up my heart,
and cried a mystic song, "My beloved, there you are!"

*

[15] A safety net of your loving care enveloped me.
I did not try to escape—captured in my wounded snare.
Satisfied that I was no prisoner, but finally free,
exhausted by my struggle, my resistance disappeared.

*

[16] Oh, the joy of this reunion, coming home.
A vagabond, a wayward soul, with no place left to go…
Right into your embrace, warm, forgiven, and atoned,
recreated, in the image of my wounded Lord!

*

[17] Bursting colors dancing all around.
No confusion or doubt, but exaltation.
I finally had let my guard come down,
and forever, I am a *new creation*!

Living in the New Creation
Reframing Your Life

> We stand upon what came before,
> the regiments of generations.
> The forward march of human corp—
> the reveille of nations.

Chapter 1

Suffering and Moral Choices

What do suffering and morality have in common? Many people make moral decisions based on values that minimize suffering. They may recognize that there is some slight utilitarian benefit to suffering, which might have some vague societal benefit. However, moral decisions and actions for many in the "culture of technology" have been relegated to an attitude of "What works for me is good for you. Each person has their moral beliefs, and if it works for some people, who am I to doubt its value?"

Pain or failure, loss, and grief make us acutely aware of human mortality; but many fail to recognize the meaning of suffering. They rely on a purely subjective layer of faith in themselves to make moral decisions. Underneath the strata of egoism and human self-protection is a pervasive sense of alienation from God that claims emancipation from the irrelevant exercise of faith.

Many think God's job in the universe is to make things work out for them. God has disappointed them because life is hard and often difficult. There is pain and suffering, poverty and war, and death. It must mean God is not so great, since I can do just as well on my own without Him.

Upholding the facade of this existential and cultural disengagement is a deep anger and frustration that God has not conformed to their expectations of His divine purpose.

The hubris of human expectations and distrust in God's goodness goes back to the Garden of Eden (Gen. 3:1–8). The devil plants the idea to Eve that God has a secret and cannot be trusted. The dirty little secret is that God does not want human beings to be on par with Him. They would discover this by eating the fruit of the tree of knowledge. They would know good and evil. They will be divine themselves and therefore would not need the crutch of obedience to God's will. The devil implies to Eve that God's secret is that obedience to Him is a sure way for God to manipulate a person. God's real intention is to protect His place at the expense of humanity's divine destiny. God is a stumbling block to human evolution and empowerment. This is the same criticism being leveled by many people today. We know from the Scriptures that this is a lie. In fact, the devil ascribes to God all of the attributes of his own disengagement from love and caring. He points the finger at God with his own pride, arrogance, and rebellion; and in so doing, he accuses God of the very malevolent intent that the devil has toward God, humankind, and all creation. The affects and consequences are that creation will, as a result of sin, fall as humanity has fallen. Now, it will grudgingly give its harvests, wrestling its abundance only through sweat and blood. Now, man and woman will suffer at the hands of creation's opposition and fight over its acquisition and resources (Gen. 3:17–20).

I have taught many classes of biomedical ethics at a local community college. I ask the question of faith and its meaning to my students every term. The opinion of many of them is that traditional religion and its values represent an antique worldview. Many believe that contemporary society has moved past these traditional norms and is formulating a new understanding of the world. Moral actions are based more on immediate gratification and subjective necessity. Traditional moral church teaching only causes conflict with the accepted moral climate and should be forgotten or marginalized. The need to formulate an attitude of compliance to the cultural need for cohesion means that opinions that differ from the cultural mandate must be bigoted, judgmental, homophobic, ignorant, closed-minded, and politically incorrect (Organista, et.al., 2018).

The new "tree of life" has become the power of modern technology and its cultural mandate of moral relativism. It's an apple from the same tree that the devil offered to Eve. We are becoming a society that does not know who or what it is. The most important question for many is what can the latest technology do to meet our wants and needs right now? The culture of technology is the culture of immediacy. We want answers now. We want information now. We want solutions to complex problems now. There are many examples of this quick-fix mentality, from our government and its corruption, the disintegration of the family, to our national debt, abortion, and euthanasia.

The institutional church is unable to confront this cultural demon of immediacy because of its own accused failures and is being culturally isolated, gobbled up, and purposely marginalized. So, when it speaks, few—if any—care to listen. Rather, the church's moral voice is muted and suppressed by the culture's discounting judgment. The old snake accuses the church saying, "I told you that you could not trust them, just like you can't trust their God."

The Christian religion is viewed, by many, as corrupted and dehumanizing. The need is obvious: to find a substitute religion that can deliver us from any moral invective to do good and avoid evil. A self-critical evaluation of a person's choices is not necessary. The immediate and pleasurable act is the right thing to do. Nothing else makes any sense to them. We can know and experience the immediate solution to problems purely through our human knowledge and wisdom. We have the low-hanging fruit of our technology to replace any outmoded idea of God or His goodness (Wisdom 15:7–19).

There is a pastoral response to the "technology culture." It requires reclaiming Christ's categorical imperative. Using the metaphor of "the vine and the branches," in John's Gospel, Jesus says, "A new commandment I give you to love one another as I have loved you" (John 15:1). This statement requires several important things: belief in the person of Christ, belief in His love for me, and belief in the same love for others. The categorical imperative of Jesus is so simple that it's hard to accept. Federal, state, and civil laws are based on principles of common law that rest on principles of natural law. We have thousands of laws that govern driving, voting, the marketplace, and criminal behavior. Jesus does not give us a library of legal statutes but a simple relational commandment. Moral decisions and actions must be placed in the context of love and caring, not power or control. All relationships (contracts and covenants) should be framed in the context of the reflexive belief in this new commandment. Belief in Jesus's love and acting in this relational context opens up the new creation. Relationships built in the love of Jesus will not extort, threaten, cheat, lie, or steal since they mirror Christ's values.

Predictability and the Deity of Technology:

Many people in our society have placed their belief in the predictability of outcomes built by human ingenuity. Cars start most of the time, buildings have water and electricity most of the time, and often medical interventions restore health. Human understanding explains some of the universe. However, because things change, they don't always perform as we hoped or expected. Car batteries fail, pipes in buildings can leak and break, and medicines can cause serious or fatal side effects. Operations can sometimes lead to complications and death. Placing faith in these things is not sufficient to deal with the suffering and pain that comes with being human.

I remember a hardship that my wife and I went through several years ago. The hospital I was working for decided to save money and do away with a paid chaplain. I found out about my dismissal two weeks before Christmas and while my wife was very sick in the hospital, the very hospital that was laying me off. It's at times like this that faith is put to the test. News about what happened got around the hospital very quickly. We had to practice faith and witness to our belief with confidence that God would care for us. Well, He did provide. The administration allowed me to keep my little office in exchange for visiting some patients. Pastoral Care Associates (PCA), which is our nonprofit corporation, received several donations that allowed the ministry to pay me for several months. I was able to spend more time with my wife and help her recover. Within a few months, new leadership took the reins at the hospital; and because I had persevered and stayed there, they gave me a new contract. However, at the time, we were put under the pressure of believing without understanding. We were compressed by circumstances to experience suffering and trust at the same time. I have had many invitations of this kind to perfect my faith. Suffering in faith softens the heart and melds it into a compassionate and tender rhythm. On the other hand, suffering with faithlessness creates a hardened heart, like the Pharaoh of Egypt's whose heart was set against the people of Israel (Exod. 8:15). Trusting, and believing, in predictable man-made outcomes in a de-transcendent way that leads to bitterness, hopelessness, anger, and fear when they fail to work. Misplaced belief causes people to bet on the world's horse only to lose the prize of meaning and virtue. Hardened hearts become less likely to care for others. They become less affected by the suffering of others and dull to the effects of their ideology on others and society. A hardened heart tends to project the harm of its own irregular heartbeat onto others. Our culture can even scapegoat the church to avoid the obvious failure of its idols of wealth, fame, self-promotion, and power. After all, the cultural elite have to blame something, or someone, for their failures to produce what they promise. It's a worldview that suffocates humanity and leaves behind only cynicism and ambiguity.

How does the Christian faith confront the misplaced belief in the deity of culture? God's nature does not change. He is always God. His love for each person is constant. He loves and gives all the time and forever. In the midst of change, personally and in the world around us, there is a steady pulse of connection that binds all things together. There is that immutable reality of God's presence that cements together matter and life. He is eternal and invites us into a relationship with Him through Jesus Christ. Belief in God, accepting His divine nature and His bond with humanity and creation, is far easier to trust in, rather than transitory and changing materiality. Those who criticize Christian believers because they need a crutch like faith in God to hold them up, fail to recognize the unsteady ground of temporality and self-delusion on which they are teetering. In Christ, we trust in a loving god who cares for us and invites us into a dynamic relationship with other people and with His gift of the new creation. Misplaced belief in the deity of culture advocates for "no God at all" because it's essential to maintain the fantasy of human divinity. It substitutes partial predictability as proof of faithless belief. The illusion of intellectual disengagement from God's caring means that the person is alone and that no one cares. This idea tends to foster a moral stance that avoids deeper self-examination and hides from a self-critical evaluation of a person's choices and his or her impact on others. It influences culture to float away from the moorings of its connection to God's purposes and His care. With no ties to real transcendence, culture is left to defend the illusion of a god of its own making, one that the cultural god makers can manipulate.

Idols are inventions of human beings. They are myths forged by human imagination. Sometimes they are just like us in form and temperament; sometimes they have combinations of both human and superhuman characteristics. In either case, they are de-transcendent. To paraphrase St. Paul, they attempt to replace the god who created the universe with gods of human creation (Rom. 1:25). We know today that ancient Romans and Greeks had technology that could make their temple idols appear to move, emit smoke, and make sounds. Technology can be used to promote a culture's myths at the expense of reality, like Hollywood's unbelievable epic heroes and fantasies today. It can even use a kind of pseudoscience to reinforce its moral ambiguity. One example is the notion that a person is born with a genetic predisposition to become gay. Many people think that God made the person that way, and they are determined by genetic factors (Nguyen, 2017)). The gay gene theory has been disavowed by the scientific community as not supportable and invalid. Yet it is widely believed by many people. Studies indicate that there are a variety of factors involved in homosexual behaviors (studies noted in *Science,* 2019). Only eighty years ago there was a so-called theory suggesting that the size of a person's cranium indicated brain capacity and intelligence. The conclusion was that races with smaller craniums were inferior (see Eugenics *notes*). Scientific misinformation today may even extend to the climate change debate. It includes some facts. However, the pantheistic religion of the global warming social agenda raises concern for Mother Earth to a level of apocalyptic proportions (American Family Association). If the good earth is to be worshiped as a god, then what need is there for redemption? All that is required is to repent and return to the place where the earth is in proper balance. Who cares about the people on the earth? They are expendable. They need to be limited by abortion or euthanasia or sterilization to minimize their carbon footprints. The manipulation of scientific facts for political or economic gain, or social restructuring, is an abuse of science. When science is coerced or manipulated for political motives, it's not science anymore—it's just propaganda.

The only way to contrast the Living God with the false gods of the technology culture is to love and care as He does. The rift is clear, when we compare the commandment that Jesus gives versus the commandments that culture and the state project. Their god exacts a high cost for de-transcendent worship. Rights that belong to the person because of God's transcendent gift of creation, namely, freedom, are appropriated by the state with utilitarian justifications by the elite and powerful. Social discourse that defends the dignity of every human person as a gift from God is dismissed as irrelevant and arcane Religion, for many, is just what is left over from a less enlightened era and just another form of cultural or racial privilege (Minarik, 2017).

Many people try to avoid all conversations that would lead to any recognition of the importance of God. I've had patients tell me, and many programs on TV promote the idea, that aliens from outer space are able to come and go on our planet. The aliens are the real gods. They made us who we are. Well, who made them? I wonder. The questions I have are "How's that working for you? Do the aliens love you? Do they care about you at all? From all I have read, all they do is abduct people and use them for experiments. Is this the best that they have to offer?" Humanity is just a sideshow of mythic semi-deities with special powers, a modern type of Gnosticism.

I know the love that Jesus has for me. He showed it on the cross. I believe His Word because He is real and not a creation of an overactive imagination. I believe Him because He rose again and lives in my heart. I believe that when He comes back to claim His bride the church, there will be no doubt about who is the Bridegroom. Jesus will not abduct us into heaven. He will be leading a parade of faithful persons who believe His Word, are saved through His death and resurrection through grace, and have a personal relationship with Him and care for each other (Rev. 21:1–5).

The delusion of our modern technological culture is that quasi-scientific myths, like the aliens and others, are meant to replace the relational god revealed in Christ. The ascent of the myths of culture and quasi-science effectively cause moral choices to be situational and subjective. As a result of this misplaced mythic belief, marriage can be redefined to include couples of the same sex. Genetic engineering and cloning, abortion, and any other scientific procedures are absolute. The belief in mythic science is the new Gnostic tree of life. The culture's god is at stake if the church denies access to any development of scientific knowledge, no matter what the moral or ethical cost. The church, when it calls into question this new divine right, must be put in its place and depicted as an obstacle to progress and moral evolution (Marx & Engels, 1969 edition).

The new cultural *de-transcendence* attempts to replace the incarnation of God and man in Christ Jesus with an anti-incarnation myth of pseudo-culture and pseudoscience. The Christian faith is in direct opposition to this new hegemony between mythic culture and mythic science. The antidote to this created cultural idol is the relational truth of the love of Jesus Christ.

The mission statement of the church has already been written: the new commandment is to love one another as Christ loves you, me, and every other person (John 15:11–12). Moral theology and ethics are centered in the heart of this relational definition. They define caring for one another as Christ Jesus cares for you and me. I am not talking about getting rid of common law. Rather, I'm pointing to a relationship of and in grace with Jesus Christ that applies to the many complications and facets of the moral choices that we face today.

The followers of these cultural gods want no part of a morality that is objective or normative. They shun the idea that values exist as goods in themselves, because they are afraid of exposing the culture's relational failure. The real place where free choice and liberty reside is in the person of Jesus Christ. He is the living new commandment. Jesus is our the personal relationship to truth. A value in the Gospel that Pilate wanted and was supposed to uphold (John 18:37–38). God's commandment "to love" is His epistemology. God's work in Christ is the proper balance of justice and mercy. We are not in fear of breaking the law if we love one another in the heart of Christ. Caring for one another in Christ is the truth, it is our life, and it is the way of freedom.

I am not opposed to science or culture. There are many wonderful people looking to understand the universe and apply our knowledge to cure sickness and other societal challenges. Culture can deepen and enhance our human interactions. I recognize the beneficent intention of quality science and a culture that supports the dignity of each person and the value of each person's life. Safeguarding the proper nature of culture, and science, is possible only when there is recognition of God's transcendence and His relational divine nature. Science and culture can move in tandem with God's creation without trying to take God's place (Kant, 1999 ed.).

Many leaders in the institutional church want to avoid the conflict of a "de-transcendent culture" by trying to demystify the Bible and explain away its transcendent truth. Cultural modernist *apologist* theologians have tried to water down the resurrection of Jesus as just a good story or metaphor. The Jesus Seminar's critical, modernist approach to the faith of the church is an example of this de-transcendence. Others have acceded to the culture's mythic utopia by accepting its denial of sin and its consequences. The real conflict and challenge facing the church is demystifying culture and science with the Gospel's proclamation of the divinity of Christ. The way to victory in the conflict is by the same means the early church used to combat the paganism of its day. The book of Acts contains this pattern: the Holy Spirit's power comes upon the apostles; it leads to the proclamation of the Gospel, which leads to the love of the brethren, which leads to suffering, persecution, redemption, and ultimate victory (Acts 2:29–43).

Proclamation is a personal testimony of what Jesus has done for me. It means knowing what I believe and why I believe it. We often think it just means speaking God's Word to others. I am not denying this element of evangelization. However, I'm the first person that the Holy Spirit has to convince of God's love. The proclamation of something means that I have experienced it. The apostles at the first Pentecost had to describe what happened to them and interpret what it meant. The church's response to the culture's mythic gods and gurus is to witness to the transforming power of the real God. There is no substitute for the proclamation of a person's conversion. When we share the story of what Christ Jesus has done for us, it clashes against our culture's mythic gods of entertainment and immediacy. It collides with its failure to produce love, change, and transformation. The culture can only offer partial political or economic benefits to its followers. It cannot produce transcendent meaning and purpose. The reason why many churches downplay conversion is they have adopted, or are collaborating with, our culture's relativistic values and want to avoid conflict with its mythic fantasy.

Pastoral care communities are centered on the proclamation that "Jesus is Lord." It witnesses to the transforming love of the Holy Spirit. In the past, the priests or ministers were supposed to be the ones with the religious experience. They were counted on to translate God's Word into action. They were relied upon by the faithful to be the example of God's involvement in the community. The pastoral care community invites every person through their baptism to articulate the experience of their conversion and its meaning. When I experience trials or sufferings, I have to hold on to the proclamation of the Word and its connection to my community. It is, at the same time, an opportunity to expand my proclamation of God's Word through the present painful or joyful situation.

Jesus prepared Himself for the hardships that He knew He would have to face (Matt. 4:1–11). The reason He talked about His suffering and death in Jerusalem was He knew His testimony about the love of the Father, and He knew what it meant. He didn't avoid the conflict with the cultic authority, nor did the early church (Mark 8:31–32). Stephen in Acts 7:1–59 is martyred, not just for what he said but for what he saw—his personal experience. His proclamation clashes with the Jewish culture. He witnesses to his vision of the divinity of Christ and the new creation. His preaching and revelation stands in sharp contrast to the Jewish interpretation of the Scriptures. They were waiting for a mythic Messiah that would free Israel from foreign domination. They expected that their Messiah would create a new political and economic theistic state. Other nations would have to deal with them. It was a creation of their own fantasy, and its defense would not allow any opposition.

The real Messiah is the "Good Shepherd" (John 10:11–17). He reveals the Father's love. He has suffered and died at our hands. He has been raised to life so that we all might live with God. Stephen witnessed to the preeminence of Jesus and in so doing smashed the Pharisaic mythic view of the Messiah. They had to kill him to defend and keep their broken myth from being exposed and disappearing (Acts 7:1–59).

The proclamation of God's Word is not just the readings on Sundays or sermons or Bible verses. It's a persons own personal relationship with Jesus Christ and what that means to you and me. Perhaps the reason we see so few signs and wonders today is we are afraid or unable to articulate our own proclamation of God's care and love.

Caring for the brethren is a commitment to a moral and ethical way of life. One of the most important elements of caring in Christ is to become conscious and self-aware of our behaviors that need to be healed and changed. Active listening training with small group support and spiritual direction is an important way to make the process of personal spiritual growth more intentional, accountable, and communal (Savage 1996).

Faith is looked upon by many as a private thing. Our culture often promotes faithlessness isolation. Cultural political correctness teaches that belief is something an enlightened person would not want to speak about. It's so private that sharing it with others is a breach of its essential character. It's so personal that it's easy to dismiss, since using it as a point of view is to have an agenda to manipulate others. It's between the person and their gods or God alone. Belief, for many, should remain hidden from our public discourse. I'm an Anglican priest, and I have sometimes thought that many mainline Protestant churches have taken out of context too literally the Scripture when Jesus said to the leper he healed, "Go and tell no one" (Mark 1:44). The opposite is true. Not only is faith an individual's personal belief, but also it contains a trust and a commitment to the community of believers and the new creation. Many people believe and promote that there has to be a great divide between personal faith and belonging to a civil society. The conflict between individual rights and the demands of the community as Tillich discussed (Tillich 1957, 1975). It's a polarity that reveals how political correctness and culture have eroded the message of the Good News and how confused society has become. Modern culture thrives on dualism, and its free-floating ethics reflects this lack of cohesion and moral center. The essential connections to the Gospel are not just in a personal faith but a communal and familial identity. The Word of God and all the sacraments are expressions of God's love and care for each person, for each family, for the entire community, and for all creation. They belong together, not separated and forced apart by the dominant culture's powerful manipulation.

> The army that guards the post,
> carries its banners on display.
> Charging with enterprise, rank, and class,
> wrapping their colors around today.

Chapter 2

The Society of False Identity and Moral Confusion

The overriding effect of modern culture's fascination with technology, its pseudo-deities and myths, is that confusion has set in about moral values and how to apply them. I teach a couple of classes on biomedical ethics at a local community college. Over and over again in every semester, I have to encourage my students just to express their opinions. I used to think that they were just immature and somewhat embarrassed about communicating their beliefs and ideas. Reading paper after paper, I began see that the issues were much deeper. They are genuinely confused about what to think, say, and feel. It's as if they are so mesmerized by the culture's expectation of political correctness that they censor themselves. It's a kind of pervasive cloud that covers any discussion. They can text to beat the band and talk about their teachers and boyfriends or girlfriends, but anything deeper causes a kind of quiet panic. Yes, there is some immaturity, but I think it's mostly confusion. I suspect that it's a hidden life commandment that says, "Nothing is as it should be, not marriage, not government, not social institutions, and not religion." It's a paralyzing and cynical truth that what they know best is confusion; and because they are so used to it, discussing spiritual values or beliefs feels foreign, unpleasant, radical, and extreme. It seems better to avoid these unpleasant topics altogether. They are left with defending their right to maintain a shallow naivete and learned helplessness. (Maier & Seligman, 2016).

I remind my students that questions like "Where did I come from?" "Who am I" and "Where am I going?" are the bases for our human journey into identity. These questions are important because the answers give a person a direction for making moral and ethical decisions. Postponing or avoiding these questions inhibits emotional and spiritual growth. I see this avoidance in so many patients in the hospital too. When I ask them about what church or religious community they attend, it's as if I am speaking a foreign language. The look on their faces seems so confused as if the question itself is something they have never thought about. If that's the case, then the question of belief and the subsequent issue of belonging to a community are outside the scope of their consideration. How does the person manage to make decisions and get through life? Many people today simply rely on the culture to provide the basis for their moral judgments. My experience as a chaplain for twenty years tells me not only is our modern culture not up to the task of providing meaning, but also, it's often behind the problem of society's narcissistic and faithless worldview. I ask my students in their papers to describe their beliefs and how they came to them. Few, if any, can articulate anything other than the questionable values of someone else, their parents, friends, or teachers or celebrities. They do so with little sense of trust or confidence. They tend to rely on what the dominant cultural beliefs are and support them as their gospel.

I had an experience that points out the power of media and culture. I lived in a neighborhood that had many light displays at Christmas. One of my neighbors had a display of ghosts and scary demons that proclaimed *The Nightmare before Christmas*. I went over to their house and rang the doorbell and asked the owner, "What do ghosts, and demons have to do with the birth of Jesus Christ our Savior?"

He said, "Don't you get it? It's from the movie."

I asked him if he would please take it down because I found it offensive, and of course, he refused. I was reminded, every time I had to round that corner, about the twisted worldview "culture" that has corrupted, and become hostile to, the gift of our redemption in Christ. I pray for the people in that house. They had to be very confused and unhappy to celebrate a sick movie instead of the incredible gift of the incarnation. Many say that the media has little or no impact on people's decisions. It's clear in this case that it has a huge impact, even larger than we know (McLuhan, 1967).

The Scriptures give us quite a different view of who we are, from the confused picture of the culture and media. We are not consumers, or masses of people, or gangs, or voting blocks, or focus groups, or different classes. We are children of God and meant to be disciples of Jesus Christ (Acts 2:37–43). Our identity is predicated on the truth of Jesus's teaching: "Love one another as I have loved you" (John 15:12). Discipleship includes suffering with the heart of Jesus Christ for the condition and confusion of the world. It's the belief that when things seem to be at their worst, God is at His best.

My wife, Dorothy, had been chronically ill for a number of years. I was amazed by her courage and her witness to the love of Jesus in the midst of her disability and pain. When she saw the doctor or had to go to the hospital, she was always more concerned about those caring for her than her own illness. Everyone who had taken care of her always asked about her and how she was feeling. She brought not only grace, but prayer with her. She was not a burden to care for. Dorothy did experience pain and the associated grief that came with her condition. She had a disciple's heart that shared a proclamation of God's love. It goes out and continues to evoke a witness though her life to the love of Jesus Christ.

The Media Is Not the Heart of the Message!

The media is not the Christian message. Television, print, radio, movies, and video games are often tools propping up the cultural deities they promote, and advertise, to maintain their mythic social agenda. The media is enamored with its power to persuade and shape beliefs. A public relations plan by the church cannot absorb the ideological assault by the media or make our culture change direction. There are too many powerful people who hate Christianity. They don't want to compete with the real God. Their gods are puny stand-ins propped up by money, programming, and advertising. The media is used as a major vehicle to promote and create the culture's easy values and false gods. Just ask yourself these questions: How many programs are predicated on violence? How many murders have you witnessed on TV or movies or video games just in one year? Is our culture teaching us, and our children, that violence is the appropriate way to solve problems? Violence or suicide is often glorified by the culture as a way out of difficult relationships or hardships and suffering. Look at how many violent programs fill the airtime. Is it any wonder that our society is becoming more angry, more fixated on immediate gratification (sex, drugs, materialism)? After all, it's where the public spends its money. The lines have blurred. Immediate gratification is promoted because it sells, or does it sell because it's promoted *(IS RA, Report on Aggression, 2018)*. They have been, and continue to traumatize our culture with death and violence.

Many of the intellectually elite have engaged in belittling the Christian faith. You can pick up newspaper editorials, tweets, and cartoons and see how Christians are being singled out for having closed minds or narrow opinions and being hypocritical. Christians are equated with Muslim extremists who kill, maim, and torture in the name of Allah. We are accused of being disrespectful of others' beliefs, being sanctimonious, and rigid. Many say, "How dare those Christians suggest that a gay person can change and become straight or that marriage is between a man and a woman. How could those Christians force their own morality on everyone else? They are so hypocritical." I've read these opinions from many of my students in their papers. Where do these ideas come from? I doubt if they are born with them. Are these opinions what they have swallowed from the media and the mythic culture's *de*-transcendent god makers? These students don't know where they got these notions of God and the church. They judge that it must be true because all their friends and many professors think and believe the same cultural propaganda and stereotypes.

Trying to change public perception of the church by using the media is like trying to have lunch with a lion and wondering why he's not interested in eating his salad. What he wants to do is to devour you! I realize that not all media professionals are like minded on the subject of religion. There are many Christians working in the field of media and promoting a positive image of Christianity. It is becoming increasingly apparent, however, that Christian films and media need to be independent from the dominant cultural worldview by developing our own creative infrastructure to present the truth of the Gospel.

The pervasive dropped-out *de*-churched cultural mindset is to view religion and its values as a hindrance to the evolution of the progressive culture and its gods. To promote the cultural anti-Christian agenda, people with money and influence support cultural evangelists who attack the church, such as Bill Maher. It's odd that no matter how few people actually watch his program on HBO, he's somehow always in front of the camera. It's a miracle of bad taste that the cultural god of ratings keeps them on the air at all. Oh, there is a god, and its name is HBO or CBS or NBC or whatever or whoever sponsors these programs or pays their salaries. There are other sages for the intellectually elite on PBS, such as Bill Moyers. They are usually interviewing someone who is the latest artist, writer, or media type that articulates the irrelevancy of Christianity. I occasionally watched *Law and Order* until I realized that if a doctor, minister, priest, or police person was involved in the case, they usually were the guilty suspect. These programs, and others, promote the cultural belief that institutions cannot be trusted. They teach that on the outside, clergy, doctors, and even the police appear good; but really, they're monsters.

The media has no problem with selling the new-age message of godless believing. They find the occult fascinating, witchcraft admirable, and astrology a science of the mind that is ageless and new at the same time. Whatever idea that will raise curiosity about the cultural mythic gods are wonderful and deeply insightful. Atheism is so smugly superior and brilliant, being freed from the encumbrance of the opiate of the people (Marx & Engles, 1969). The greatest perpetrators of murder and death in the history of the world were Mao, Stalin, and Castro. All were all atheists, and so was Hitler who developed his own mythic superhuman gods.

The message that the media and pseudo-culture intone sounds something like this:

"Those poor backward Christians, they just need to be liberated from the constraints of religion and do homage to our superior cultural enlightenment. If they could just accept this political and cultural evolution, then they too can be freed from the past and sent on the journey of liberation, self-realization, and cultural fulfillment."

The media is spearheading this sectarian campaign; and for many people, who actually believe this phony story, it leads to a wide path of failure and deceit. The gods they're promoting are entertaining, full of special effects, heroes who never die, and myths that draw us back to Baal (1 Kings 18:18–39). They will not love you or anyone for that matter. They will only embrace your money and will never feed your soul. They will leave a person lonely and isolated. Their gods will take whatever we are willing to give and never return a kind word. Belief in the media's gods will leave a person without a community, like a towel thrown on the floor in the corner of a locker room after the game is over. No one will care, and no one will notice.

Many Christians today are content to watch an evangelist on TV instead of attending church, even if they are physically able. They give money and encourage their friends to tune in. I have these questions rise up inside me when a patient informs me that they religiously watch Christian TV.

"So you are here in the hospital with a serious condition. Where is the TV evangelist? Have they come to visit you? Have they been here to hold your hand or to pray with you?" They have been willing to promise a "name it and claim it" cultural, religious materialism and reap its benefits. What will happen when the day of suffering or persecution comes?

The truth is that the false gods of culture have infected the religious climate. Many accept the notion that a person can be spiritual without community. Their belief does not include belonging to a church. They think that a relationship with Jesus does not translate to a relationship with other believers. Many Christians have removed themselves from the game and are content to watch from the sidelines, rather than engage in the vital life of Christian discipleship and community. The church is all the weaker when one person disengages from ministry. That's why the culture minimizes church involvement, or actively hinders it.

The heart of the Gospel is the gift of belonging to Jesus Christ as His child and being in His family. It stands in sharp contrast to the mythic gods of the liberal culture. Christians are not left to their own devices to find the truth. Jesus is the truth. His commandment "to love one another as He loves us" (John 13:34–35) is relational and caring. Christians don't seek the acceptance of the culture to find a measure of security. We find our security in the person of Jesus Christ. He saves us from sin and death. Believers in Christ respond to this wonderful gift of salvation by caring for others. The world covets the freedom of the sons and daughters of Jesus Christ. The cultural gods that seem so appealing dole out their favors only to a few, and only for a short time. They sparingly give out morsels of fame, money, and power only to take them back. The true God withholds nothing from us. He gives us eternal life and pours out His benefits forever. He gives us His love in the Spirit and acceptance into His family though the atonement of Jesus on the cross for our sins. The gods of the media cannot measure up. They have no real hope to give, nothing eternal to believe in, and no personal relationship with their mythic gods to offer. The best they can give is the gluttony of entertainment and its gratification of the senses, which inevitably leads to boredom. The contrasts between their worldview and the Christian worldview are legion.

The pastoral care community is an expression of the heart of Christ Jesus and His Gospel. It's one of the effective ways that Christians can confront the mythic gods of culture. We are not alone; Jesus said, "I am with you always to the end of the age." And again, "Do not be afraid little ones I have overcome the world" (John 16:33).

> Oh, the colossal carnage of daily battle,
> the roar of conflict upon the earth.
> Drumbeats of sorrow, death's saber rattles—
> the noise of strife signals our curse.

Chapter 3

A Disciple's First Choice / Mary's Choice

The decision to be a disciple begins with a yes to God. Our consent to God's calling to follow Him is the basis for all good choices. Our affirmation in baptism and the ascent of accepting Jesus as our Lord and Savior impels the believer forward into God's heart. I know that for some, this may seem obvious or even trite. However, to move on the road to discipleship, we have to start with this important first step; and it always begins with a fiat (yes). Once this choice is made, it colors all other choices.

Mary said yes to God; it presupposes God's yes to her and to His people. This yes is the Word that was made flesh "full of grace" so that God's redemption could begin its gestation and birth (Luke 1:26–38). Mary's yes affirms God's Word to Israel, God's promise of a Messiah, and God's covenant with our humanity. Our yes to our Father's invitation to love Him grafts us to His redemptive gift. Our yes to God makes it possible to contrast the real god from any false mythic cultural imitation.

The incarnation of Jesus reveals once and for all the sanctity of human life. Jesus is born through the same process of pregnancy that all human beings go through. Each stage builds upon itself a resonant sound of the Word. Jesus's conception, gestation, and birth usher in the new creation. This is what God's plan looks like through the lens of

His redemption. Mary's participation is a witness, like the prophets of the Old Testament, to God's purpose of reclaiming everything violated by our sin. The prayer she says resounds with the glorious exaltation of the music of union with God and with the new creation: "My spirit proclaims the greatness of the Lord" (Luke 1:46). When a violinist plays a solo part of a symphony, it still remains part of the symphony. Mary, the first disciple, takes in the Word of God and shelters Him in her womb; and as Luke says, "She treasured all these things and pondered them in her heart" (Luke 2:19–20). So we likewise treasure Jesus the Word of God and His works and gifts in our lives through His grace in the Spirit and ponder the Father's love in our hearts.

Dorothy and I eloped when we married. We had a long drive to Las Vegas in my little sports car across the desert. We were taking a big risk, since most of our friends and family thought that our relationship would not last. They thought we were acting out of infatuation, throwing away our future. I became very aware, during this journey, of the nature of consent. It didn't matter what others thought or said or believed. It mattered what Dorothy and I believed, and what we said. Would we have enough faith to trust our promise to each other? Would we let the voices of others, and their opinions, or disapproval, set our course apart? Would we stand together and say yes to each other and risk all the dangers of an unknown future? Well, we were happily married for thirty-four years, and we had our marriage blessed in the Episcopal and Roman Catholic Churches. I hold our choice and commitment in my heart today. When times are hard and I face challenges of health or financial stress or other kinds of pain, I remember that drive in the desert. I continue to love and hold her memory dear, because I know what it means to say yes. I know that we said yes, and I still hold precious that journey in the desert to love and care for others as we loved and cared for each other.

A disciple lives out the commitment of a graced pattern of consent to God's Word and work. A decision to follow Jesus is not a one-time choice that is added to the pile of other options. It's not a decision that has little effect because it requires just a small momentary halt to our fascination with our own goals. It's not a temporary respite from the attraction to ambition or fame. Real consent to Jesus Christ as Lord and Savior is pondered in the heart and placed in the tension of choices that can often be in conflict with the false idols of pseudo-culture. It is a yes to care for one another as Jesus cares for us (Bonhoeffer, 1995 edition).

When we think of consent, we usually think of an agreement to do or be something, to buy a car, to accept a job, to build a friendship, or to be married. The foundation of civil society rests on the ability to secure contracts by the free consent of both parties. We accept the fact that consent has to be free from coercion and that both parties have to know all the facts involved in the agreement; they have to be competent and conscious and aware of the consequences of their choice. They have to be willing, and able to the best of their ability, to fulfill the expectations of their agreements. Without this belief and trust, society would crumble and disintegrate.

We have three children. My wife and I gave them parental direction, when they were growing up, to teach them about their choices. One of the responsibilities of loving parental guidance is to keep the child from making a choice that could be harmful, since they lack life experience and maturity. Guiding the child to make healthy decisions is the responsibility of the parents. They should know from their life experience, from their education, and from God's Word what are the best choices. They expect to be obeyed since they act in the best interest of the child. One of the reasons for parental guidance is to provide for the youngster a sound basis for moral action. They come to discover and understand the nature of consent through religious training and its application. Discipline is the practical experience of the meaning of consent. Discipline, like discipleship, develops a pattern of recognition of the nature of choice and its consequences, duties, and responsibilities. That day will come, all too soon if I may add, when they will make their own adult decisions and set their own direction.

Jesus questions the apostles in the Gospels to see if they recognize the nature of His calling and theirs: "Who do you say that I am?" (Mark 8:27–30). It's the essential question of the Gospel of Mark, a question that every believer has to answer for themselves. It's a question of consent. If we answer that Jesus is the Messiah, the Son of God, we are saying yes to everything that He has done to save us. Jesus encourages us through His consent to the incarnation, atonement on the cross, and resurrection to say yes (Matt. 5:37). St. Paul says it this way in 2 Corinthians 1:19–

23, "The Son of God, the Jesus that we proclaimed among you—I mean Silvanus and Timothy and I—was never Yes and No: with him it was always Yes, and however many the promises God made, the yes to them all is in him. That's why it is 'through him' that we answer Amen to the praise of God. Remember it is God himself who assures us all, and you, of our standing in Christ and has anointed us, marking us with his seal and giving us His pledge of the Spirit that we carry in our hearts." God's Spirit affirms this yes and through grace leads us into a life of service.

Our eldest daughter before her last year of high school had decided that she wanted to serve our country and join the Navy. My wife and I were supportive of her choice. She had really thought through the decision. We were proud of her determination and her willingness to leave home and risk an unknown life in the military to serve our nation. I was an assistant priest in a mid-sized town in Texas. Several of our very close friends in the parish heard of our daughter's decision. They told us how she should be going to college and how we were not looking out for her. They refused to even let us visit them anymore and shunned us at church. It was painful to lose these friends and to hear their complaints echoed by several other parishioners. One Sunday our Episcopal bishop and his wife came to visit the parish. My wife and I were chatting with them after mass, and we told them about our daughter's decision and how proud we were of her. The bishop's wife told everyone in earshot that she had proudly served in the Navy and that is where she met her husband. It was a totally unexpected and surprising affirmation.

Once we make our yes to Jesus Christ, then God's affirmation blesses us. Once we accept God's gift of salvation, God's personal affirmation in our soul can birth endless possibilities for good. Many people think that human beings can be and do good things on their own. They think that we can build with science and technology a world of human affirmation based on ourselves, our good sense, and the power of our creative energy. Such a delusion can become a yes only to our hubris and folly. It leads to an elitist view of the world that excludes its designer and creator. They try to explain away and deny the person of God by affirming themselves without Him. The Gospels, on the other hand, show us that once we have said yes to His calling, God's Word affirms us. Jesus's baptism (Mark 1:9–13), the calling of the apostles (Luke 3:13–19), and the healing of the blind man (John 9:1–41) are examples. That is why everything depends on this yes to God the Father, for without it, we are left with only the transitory and often capricious affirmation of human judgment. It's from this focal point that we can begin to explore the meaning of morality and its resultant ethical choices.

The target we aim to identify as sound, ethical, moral action has in its heart our consent yes to the person of Jesus Christ and a willingness to follow where He leads. The ability to make good choices blossoms from this most important choice. We live in the glory of this yes forever. Likewise, sound moral teaching in the church is built on the foundation of consent to Jesus Christ. Without it (Mary's fiat, Luke 1:26–38), there would be no incarnation and therefore no redemption and no church.

Philosophy today is often a grab bag of systems built mostly on principles that tend to neglect the moral underpinnings of faith in God. Jesus's own moral action is based not on abstract patterns of immediacy, but on the concrete meaning of choices in relationship to the Father's pattern of love. Consent, to be meaningful and purposeful, has to be in relationship to someone. Jesus points to the Father as the basis for His choices: "Man cannot live by bread alone but by every word that flows from the mouth from God" (Matt. 4:4). Jesus's consent to the Father's purposes bears fruit in His ministry. He reminds the disciples that good fruit is produced from a good tree. He talks to them about how bad or good fruit cannot be disguised for long; we will know what kind of harvest it is by the fruit that it produces (Matt. 7:15–20). The qualities of goodness come from a heart that has taken up its cross and followed Jesus to Calvary (Matt. 10:38–40). The Christian view of moral decision-making is not based on a series of abstract philosophical ideas or constructs that vie for political or economic control or power. Christian moral teaching is based on the person Jesus Christ.

When He says, "Come and follow me and I will make you fishers of men" (Luke 5:10–11), Jesus is inviting the apostles to consent to a lifelong journey of following, to a life of relationship with one another. He invites them to a life of relying on His Word even when the pressures to abandon the faith are attractive. The book of Acts of the Apostles was written to encourage the church to stand firm and be courageous against the false gods of Roman culture and pagan worship. It reveals to us the price of following Jesus and the nature of consent to God's calling (Bonhoeffer, 1995 edition).

Christian moral theology is wedded to pastoral care. When Jesus is confronted with moral choices, it's usually because someone has a need. Jesus's healing on the Sabbath reveals the choice that Jesus makes between strictly keeping the Sabbath as a demand of religion or deciding to be the Sabbath, and be in the new creation, which is the time of rich blessing of God's restoration, forgiveness of sin, and release from sickness and demonic oppression. Jesus has a new kind of authority because He is so caring. His authority is not puffed up with pretentious, self-serving religious piety; rather, it points to freedom, pardon, and peace. We see, hear, and feel in the Gospels the choices Jesus and the early church made. Examples would be the woman caught in adultery (John 8:1–11) or the Good Samaritan story (Luke 10:25–37) or Jesus eating with sinners (Luke 5:27–31). We can examine the patterns of Jesus's choices. We can recognize how our choices should mirror His moral actions. The fulcrum of decision-making resides within the fabric of time. Our history, and God's redemption in Christ, presses us forward into the *new creation* (Von Balthasar, 2010 ed.).

> We stand and wait for Him to come again.
> When the trumpet will sound taps,
> and all the wars and hate will end,
> and we will bivouac in God's camp.

Chapter 4

Time-Out

The first thing a doctor does is to take the patient's history. It's a detailed description of the patient's experience of their illnesses, operations, medications, and symptoms. A history also includes diagnoses from other doctors and special information like tests. It includes the person's impressions of what might be the cause of their sickness. The history produces a pattern in the doctor's mind of how the patient got to this crisis or health concern. It also provides background information that might help with treating the complaint.

My history is an essential component of my identity. It's more than the facts of my life; it contains the underlying reasons for my previous choices. We write history to keep a record of actions and words that fill out the tablets of time. Without history, there wouldn't be any civil society because we wouldn't have any connection with the past and nothing upon which to build relationships. God's creation contains within it the history of its development. Geologists, for example, by studying rocks and geological formations can read the history stored in these objects and identify how the earth was formed. They know with some certainty when the last ice age was or how the continents were shaped. Each science, like a person, has a history that describes the past. History helps push us forward just as science explores new theories and develops new technology. Every atom or subatomic particle has a history and a place in the universe.

Every person resonates with a familial and historical context. The universe sings out the wonder of its creation by witnessing its history in the stars, in the galaxies, in the waves of the sea, or the in waves of light. God the Father who created nature is telling His story for us to feel, hear, and see. The cosmology of the universe reveals God's love. He gives creative attention to the smallest details even down to the cells that make up the hairs of our heads. We see His glory in the immense universe that is spread out before us. We feel the passion of His creative energy and the profound harmony of the physical laws that govern the matter and form of God's engagement with His creation.

God being outside of time does not have a history; only the created universe contains a record of God's engagement with matter. Time can be measured by a clock, the rising and setting of the sun, and the seasons of the year. God has no such measurements. He is not tied down to materiality, length, size, shape, or dimension. God is omnipresent and omniscient in part because He is not in time and not limited by its passing. He presides over all things at each and every moment. Creation is all present, now and always. We are told in the Old Testament that no one could see God and live (Exod. 19:16–24). It's precisely because God's nature is perfect and outside of time that it would be impossible for us to see Him and exist in time.

One of the wonderful gifts of the incarnation is that God now has a history. In the Old Testament, God worked through limited means: imperfect men and women, like Moses who stuttered, Job who disobeyed, and Jeremiah who felt seduced into being a prophet, just to name a few. Jesus is God and man; and as such, He is the bridge, not just between God's holiness and our sinfulness, but between God's timeless nature and our mortality. Jesus enters our time so that through Him we may enter into God's eternity. Redemption in Christ does not just save the people around at His death and resurrection, a few friends, and apostles. Jesus enters our history through the gate of materiality. Jesus enters our time so that through Him we may enter into God's family. He redeems everyone who ever existed and those who have yet to be born. Jesus told the apostles that He had to go so that the Holy Spirit could come (John 16:5–11).

The Holy Spirit that brought His body to life forever is given to us to bring the church to life. The animating gift of the Holy Spirit regenerates us in baptism and brings us into God's timeless glory. The Holy Spirit in reconciliation puts our sins in the well of God's forgetfulness. The same Holy Spirit that makes the gifts of bread and wine into the body and blood of Jesus in the Eucharist brings us into eternal communion with God (Von Balthasar, 2010).

I enjoy watching and playing basketball. I have noticed that when the game is very close, more anxiety and intensity is produced as the game clock ticks down. How many minutes remain in the game? How many time-outs do we have? Do we intentionally foul someone so that the clock will stop, and we might get another shot before time expires? Generally, it's true that the more anxious or stressed we are, the more we are aware of time. We have the idea that because time is limited and often defined by its edges, we say things like "Time is running out" or "Time is money" or "I don't have time for that" or "Time is a wasting."

Have you ever had the experience when the day just drags along and you find yourself constantly looking at the clock, wishing it would move faster? Pain tends to bring with it the slow-moving train of suffering that makes time crawl along. I once went deep-sea fishing with my dad and a lot of other people. When our boat hit the open water, I was so seasick. I think that it was the longest night of my life. I just tried to hang on till morning, hoping that I would somehow get used to the motion of the boat. I was so glad when we got to the shore, and I could be relieved of the constant nausea.

Time can be seen as flying by, for example, when I've been working intently on a project or task and would get so lost in it that I wonder, where did the time go? About ten years ago, I was the spiritual director of a Cursillo for men (a three-day retreat), and I was scheduled to give the talk on the sacraments. The presentation usually lasts an hour or two. There is a rather detailed schedule to maintain, and just so much time is allotted for this section. Well, the presence of God fell on that group, and I talked to them for seven hours. They were so blessed that even though I told them several times we had to move to the next activity, they just clamored for more teaching. Finally, the rector of the retreat said that we need to break for dinner. He had let me go on for all that time. The group and I had experienced what happens when God's holiness and His Spirit bless His people. Seven hours felt like a blink of an eye.

The end of a Cursillo is marked by a time of witnessing to your family and friends about what happened to you on the weekend. Over and over again the men stood up and shared their conversion to Jesus and how for seven hours, time seemed to stand still. Again and again, the Scriptures tell us stories when people lost a sense of time because of the experience of Jesus's teaching (Luke 9:10–15). The prayer of contemplation is like the suspension of time, in the Spirit. We are raised up into the love of God. Abiding in the Father's love is like that vision of Isaiah where He touches our lips with eternity (Is. 6:6–9). He softens our hearts from the rigors of time and the demands of worry and anxiety. He places in our hearts through His grace the rhythm of His new creation. We respond in the Holy Spirit and embrace His history of our redemption in Christ. Our society has become obsessed with time. We eat fast food. We drive fast cars. We have short conversations by texting. We hurry to get everything done in a day so that we can relax and start the fast-paced intensity all over again tomorrow. Our opening line is often "I would have…but I was so busy." The faster we go, the less time we seem to have. We feel the trap of time's fleeting abandonment. You would think that with modern technology like computers and cell phones we would have more leisure time. It seems to be just the opposite. Time is something that we feel ownership about. I have to spend my time wisely, like a commodity. I only have so much of it, and I need to make the most of the limited time I have. Time is also something that can be robbed or taken from us. It's fleeting and easily lost or wasted. The idea that time is a gift from God is only something we think about after a close call on the freeway. Am I suggesting that we go back to the horse and buggy or retreat to some place of isolation from modern communication? No, of course not, but I am saying that we need to see the issue and gauge its effect on us and the church.

Many churches have added to the pressure of time constraints by scheduling more and more activities. The breathless pursuit of more and more programs leaves no time to reflect. I think that we need a time-out in Christ. The church can be a place of resetting our inner clock to match the movement of God. It can be a place where we put the culture's alarm clock away with its breathless fascination with busyness and focus on being together in Jesus. The church needs to move at a decidedly different pace than our culture with its grinding demands. The church year is the basis for the cycle that can bring us into step with God's tempo. So often we march through the church calendar as much to get through it so we can move on to the next thing. The financial pressure at Christmas or Easter is predicated by the culture's appropriation of our symbols to manufacture a materialistic deity rather than the real God of love. Christianity has been seduced into accepting this foreign substitute of snowmen, or Santa, Easter rabbits and Easter eggs. Christians need to recover not just the meaning of the seasons of the church year but the tempo and timing of them. I have to confess that I have been guilty, at times, of getting caught up in the cultural enjoyment of the seasons. I have sometimes missed experiencing the pattern of God's redemption with all the seasons' cultural demands. I've had that experience of not being ready for Lent or Advent because I have been too busy to think about them. Within the cycle of the church year, there is a resonance of the timing of God the Father's redemptive plan. It causes me to enter into my own identification with my history and God's gift of salvation. The historical themes of Jesus and His life, His birth, His family, and His travels as a boy to Jerusalem are not disconnected from my own experience. I too was born, lived in a family, and traveled with my parents. It points to the rhythm of birth, life, death, and resurrection in Jesus Christ.

It is absolutely true that someday life for me on this planet will end. I visit patients who are very sick, and some are dying. I come face-to-face with my own mortality every time I minister to them or their families. It reinforces a kind of anchor for me that time eventually will run out. Some people say that thinking about the reality of the shortness of life and its fragility is morbid. I think just the opposite; it can provide an awareness of the importance of every moment and every choice. Our mortality should not be a surprise. Yet many people are overwhelmed when they briefly rub up against it.

Our culture is fascinated by death and at the same time repulsed by it. Television and movies love to act out death, murder, and violence. We know that after the show is over, the actors get up and go on with their lives. Somehow, we have the notion that time will not really run out for us. We will just get up and keep going when we are faced with sickness. We unconsciously believe that we will be rescued from the reality of our death, and the consequences of our compulsions and the ravages of time. Our culture unfortunately will do almost anything to promote our existential avoidance.

I once got a call from the hospital about a middle-aged man who had died in the emergency room. The medical team had done all they could, but they could not resuscitate him. The wife was hysterical with grief, and the staff felt that I should come to provide spiritual support. I went there and was directed by the staff to the patient's room. I sat across from her dead husband who was lying on a hospital gurney. I introduced myself and expressed my sympathy at her loss. She began to yell and scream for him to wake up. Usually this kind of denial lasts for a few minutes. It takes time to let the reality of the loss settle into a person's consciousness. She continued to go on like this for over an hour. I finally had to tell her in a very clear voice while I looked directly into her face, "I am sorry, but your husband is never going to wake up in this life. He is dead, and nothing is going to change that sad fact. I am sorry that he died. It's going to require difficult days ahead of change and grief. It's very sad and painful." I don't think that I had ever been so direct to a grieving person before. It seemed to help her, and she began to admit to herself that he had really died.

Many people are so ill-prepared to face their human limitations. I remember working with a family whose father had a huge stroke, and they asked me with all seriousness, "Can't they do a brain transplant?"

I asked myself, *Hmm, I wonder who in this family would be a good candidate?*

Our culture sets up a mythic scientific salvation only to be hit in the face with its inevitable failure. Doctors usually have an idea of their limitations. They usually have been around enough death to understand its permanence and not to be surprised when time runs out. Our modern society is not interested in establishing limits to behavior. You can drink, do drugs, and smoke or do any other compulsion that suits your lifestyle. I often wonder if all the overdoses and toxic alcohol abuse, all the sexual diseases, and other self-inflicted compulsions could magically disappear, if there would be any patients at all in the hospital. If you really wanted to cut down on the cost of health care, cutting down on self-destructive behavior would do it.

I have had patients ask me, after admitting that they smoked two packs of cigarettes a day for thirty years, "How could God do this to me and give me lung cancer?" Many people never give God a thought until a tragic situation arises. How can a person be concerned with the real God when they are busy creating a god that supports and condones their habits and lifestyle? When we create a god of our own image, we don't even need to talk to it; we have ourselves to be concerned about. I visited a patient who told me he didn't need to go to church to talk to God (boy, I have never heard that one before) and that he talked to God when he went to the mountains.

I asked him, "When was the last time you went to the mountains and talked to God?"

He giggled and said, "Oh, about ten years ago."

It's important that Christians live believing the message of the apocalyptic writers that time is short. Don't waste your time lubricating the culture's self-interest and worshiping a solitary god that requires that you drive one hundred miles to talk to Him. The real God meets us where we live right in our hearts.

The church has gone through two thousand years of history to arrive at this moment in time. It's not an accident that we have a tradition built on the faith and witness of others. The book of Revelation affirms the witness of the "company of martyrs" who worship the Lamb around the throne of God (Rev. 7:9–16). Their time of testing is over, but ours is not. The time of suffering and persecution has not ended. The fullness of time is emerging through the church's testimony. It reveals and echoes the "bride's" eternal praise to God (Rev. 21:1–5). The Christian community has not always lived a history of faithfulness to its calling in Christ Jesus. The book of Revelation criticizes churches that may posture in a Christian style but are not rooted in an authentic witness to Christ. The same indictment may well apply to many in the modern church. We are to guard against acquiring a fascination with the culture at the expense of proclaiming the Gospel. What makes the book of Revelation so profound is its relevance to our present situation. The author reminds us that time is running out. It has been for two thousand years, and its approaching speed is the speed of the sound of a trumpet (Rev. 8:6–7).

One of the effects of our witness to Jesus Christ is a recognition that His Father is in charge of time. He's not a big watchmaker in the sky who winds up the cosmos and lets it go. He's not just involved intimately in its construction but engaged in every part of it. History is not just a litany of facts. It does more than describe wars, governments, discoveries, dangers, toils and sacrifices, victors, and losers. History is going in a direction. It's a movement through time that reveals our values, our character, and our proclamation of Christ's redemption forever. Each one of us has a unique part to play in the redeeming of time as it sweeps forward. Our individual history is important in bringing in that eternal day that dawns when time ends. Until that day comes and from today and through tomorrow, looking back and looking ahead, in the present moment, in prayer and fasting, in reconciliation and absolution, and in caring for and serving one another, we celebrate the time God gives us so that someday we will live without it.

> Till that day arrives, we balance the time,
> and center our optics on that future day,
> ambivalent, half there or left behind,
> still vainly trying to brush the past away.

Chapter 5

A Mission to Care

Jesus sent out the seventy-two to do the same things He was doing. They were to use His name at their "calling card" (Luke 10:1–10). We see this sending out as a dress rehearsal of the sending out of the apostles by the Spirit after Pentecost. The missionary zeal of the early church was motivated by the heart of Jesus to care for the lost. The primary reason we have a proclamation is tied to our experience of the pastoral care and love of Jesus Christ. To be a missionary is to bring the message of God's care, salvation, and redemption to those who don't know about this gift. We have been taught to think that missionaries are sent only to foreign lands. The real question is how to bring the Gospel to our modern culture that resists a personal encounter with the Living God. The heart of the Gospel is caring, and if we fail in caring, then we will fail in mission.

America is on the brink of losing its spiritual anchor in Christ. If the trend continues to move toward a completely secular society rooted to nothing but human folly, then the church will have to stand empowered by its proclamation. I think that we are not so much in an emerging church, as some have said, but a remnant church that will be more attached to the Bridegroom—a church much like the early church whose model was a life shared in discipleship. It emerged two thousand years ago and burst upon the scene in the pagan culture of that day. It had a zeal that changed the world. The Acts of the Apostles and St. Paul's writings tell us what they did and how they did it. Christians today from countries like Rwanda and the Middle East and other places of persecution understand the suffering of being tested and purified for the sake of the kingdom of God. Missionaries are those who are suffering all over the world because of their faith in Jesus Christ as Lord and Savior. We see the pastoral heart of Jesus on display in the experience of persecution for the sake of the Gospel (2 Cor.11:16–30).

Not long ago I had received a newsletter from our group, the Anglican Church, in the Americas that it was decided that there would be a goal to establish one thousand new churches. The first thing that happened was we had a big fight over who is in charge. The next thing that happened was congregations and clergy decided to join other Anglican groups. My Anglican community that started with three hundred congregations and aspired to plant one thousand new congregations had dwindled to only one hundred congregations. I praise God for this apparent failure. It has put us right in the path of being a remnant people. God's glory is not based on buildings or financial security. It would have been far better for us to have decided to train and equip with prayer and support one hundred new disciples that would have changed the world. Look across Europe and Canada; they built a lot of wonderful churches with grand artwork and architecture. People come from all over the world to see them. Once the crowds of tourists leave, they are empty. The Word of God is not planted in buildings but in hearts. Jesus is not going to ask us how many church buildings we constructed in His name. He is going to ask us a much more telling set of questions at our judgment. I think the Scriptures direct us to His heart of caring for one another. Believe me, I love to celebrate at church and lead its liturgy. Still, a church building can be a lonely place when everyone goes home for the day. A heart dedicated to God's love in the Spirit is never empty. It's full of grace and truth. A heart of service to Jesus is not lonely but full of opportunities to care for others. The heart of a disciple is on a daily mission of proclamation of the Gospel of Christ. There is no substitute for a dedicated disciple. Buildings, programs, mission statements, and all the stuff churches do can be only busy work. They don't begin to make the impact on the culture that one trained disciple can make (Lessard, 2017).

The heart of the Gospel is not a commodity on sale at a bargain basement price. It's not going to cost you just a tithe or a well-run stewardship program. The kingdom of God is the "pearl of great price" (Matt. 13:45–46). We must be willing to share and invest everything so that we can buy the field. It is not enough to claim to have found the "pearl" somewhere. We must have ownership of it and have it secured with a "deed of trust." Ownership removes all doubt about who has rights to the property and to the wealth that the property contains. We have been given the pearl of salvation in Christ through His death and resurrection. It's secured for us by a deed of trust in the Spirit. It's written in our hearts through baptism. The going price is not based on a fair exchange of equal value, my life in exchange for Christ's life. I am not worthy in comparison to the value of the giver of the gift, "God's own Son." It's beyond anything I can give, because He is the giver. He is the gate through which we pass into that eternal country, the new creation of Christ's redemption (Jn. 10:7–10).

The new creation is conveyed by the words of Jesus on the cross: "Father, forgive them, they know not what they do" (Luke 23:34). These reconciling words on the cross make and give you and me the connection to the Father's domain. Without these words, we would be trapped, unable to possess any rights as God's sons and daughters. These words come right from the Father's heart to us. We are cared for and loved by God so intensely that He offers it for free, not because it's of little value or of low interest, but because it is far above any treasure. The gift and the cost to the giver are priceless. No one can afford to repay or purchase with any amount of money or gold or jewels what God's Son has given to us. "Caring for one another like Christ cares for us" includes giving as part of our calling into God's family. Christian giving far exceeds the Old Testament tithe. Jesus did not hold anything back to save us on Calvary. Once we know the gift and its cost, we can respond with joy and share His love with the people around us. God's kingdom is missionary because it is caring. God's new creation is missionary because it is freely given and priceless. His new creation is our life in service to others.

Recently I was called by the hospital staff to visit a young woman who was going to give birth to her second stillborn child. She was quite upset and grieving. I listened to her story as she told me how much she wanted this child. In her first pregnancy, she was not careful and maintained a lifestyle that had put the child at risk, and she lost it. She was determined to change the outcome in this pregnancy. She had left her so-called friends behind and had been sober and careful to follow the doctor's recommendations. She had cleaned up her life to prepare for motherhood and this new child. I listened to her pain and disappointment. She asked, "How could God put me through this again when I have done everything this time to care for this baby?" I listened through her tears and sorrow; then came that pause, the moment she needed someone to put this loss in some kind of spiritual context, to give it some kind of meaning. I said to her, "God has given you two beautiful gifts. Their lives have caused you to change your destructive habits and friends to live a new life." I noted that "only love can do that; only love can bring about a change like that to wholeness and hope. Love like that never dies. Your children have given you a gift that you will always possess. They have given you new life and brought the gift of meaning and love into your heart. Even though their lives had been short, they had placed in your heart the grace of a mother's love."

I continued, "It's true that both of these losses are painful and sad. You're going to be grieving the loss of what could have been. Please don't forget that when the sadness lays heavy on your heart, remember the incredible gift they have given to you now and forever."

God's grace and love are particularly available in times like these. Funerals are important moments of pastoral care and are filled with meaning. It was at a funeral that Jesus raised Lazarus from the dead (John 11:1–44). The story of the widow of Nain in Luke 7:1–10 tells us about when Jesus brought back to life the only son of a grieving mother. This story is like Jesus. He too is the only son of a widowed mother. We see in this picture a rehearsal story of the resurrection of Jesus. These moments of mortality and grief are opportunities to translate redemptive meaning into an event that can easily be seen as annihilation. The gift of caring reflects the deeper context of life, and that's what Jesus does in the Scriptures. In John 3:1–21, He tells Nicodemus that he must be born again. He provides a new map of reality that is representative of the new creation. Jesus recasts meaning within the construct of the Father's love. It is the love of the Father that provides the eternal relationship with

Him. Similarly, caring in the heart of Jesus will reshape the Word and the sacrament of the moment into a new creation that leads us from darkness into His light.

Caring as Jesus cares causes us to "listen with His intention and speak with His heart." Jesus gives us the language in the Holy Spirit to interpret the meaning of the event with its proper ethical/moral and theological pattern. The gift of this holy translation of meaning brings us back to the movement of abiding in Christ (Jn. 15:1–17).

The person becomes aware that the event, they are going through, is far more transcendent than they thought. The experience, no matter how painful, is pregnant with meaning and value. The Divine Mystery can be lost if there is no one to help decode the experience into the context of abiding in the new creation with Christ. I am not talking about pawning off some religious platitude to avoid being touched by a person's pain. I am speaking of listening to the person's pain and responding, when appropriate, with a gentile attitude of caring and sensitivity in the Spirit and sharing its redemptive meaning.

I have studied theology. I have plodded through many dry and intellectual tomes that are considered great theological books. The greatest theological lessons I have learned have been from real moments when pain, suffering, joy, and exaltation are translated by God's Holy Spirit straight from God's heart. It's a precious moment of blessing when God's Spirit moves to help someone see the holy significance of their experience (Tounier, 1957). The living theology of grace is inside the present event. It's not just an intellectual exercise. It's a shared experience that reveals meaning and value in God's terms. It's illuminating and revealing, and it leads to love of God and neighbor. Living theology is real theology because it's so grounded in every moment and in everything.

Jesus reminded the apostles that He would go to Jerusalem and suffer at the hands of the chief priests, suffer and die, and be raised up again (Matt. 18:21–22). Was He being morbid or promoting some self-fulfilling prophecy? I think He was translating the meaning of the events that would soon overtake Him and them. He wanted them to recognize the deeper implications and the transcendent purpose of God's plan of redemption. His death might look like a failure to everyone else. He knew that the religious establishment saw Him as just another false prophet who could do some spectacular tricks, but in the end, He dies nailed to the tree of disappointment. The apostles must not be taken in by the fabrication of the world's view of His purpose. They must remember the words He spoke to them and their experience of Him. Jesus reshapes the power of death on the cross into the power of God's redemption in the resurrection. He restructures disappointment and disillusionment into God's plan of salvation. Like on the road to Emmaus (Luke 24:13–35), Jesus translates the meaning of the events of Holy Week. He tells them of the spiritual plan of the Father to bring all things into Christ. He invites us to share in this ministry of reconciliation and its translation through caring for one another as He cares for us. The experience of participating in this living theology is validated by the fruits of the Holy Spirit. The translation of caring as Jesus does comes from the heart of God's love, and it produces loving outcomes. It's easy to tell if the translation of the event fits within God's love language. The person receiving it responds with a release from pain, doubt, and shame or guilt. It catches us off guard because it is so simple, right, loving, and freeing. It's the kind of theology that the disciples shared with Jesus as they headed down the road to Emmaus. He came alongside them and in the midst of their grief and sorrow, fear, and doubt. He explained the Scriptures to them, that the Messiah must suffer and die and rise again. They wanted to hear more. This man could make sense of it all. Their hearts burned within them. Hope was being born, and their faith was renewed. Finally, when they ate with Him and He broke the bread, they could see Him. It took a translation of God's mighty power to reveal the meaning of the resurrection and their resulting communion, and it opened up God's new creation right there.

Modern secular culture often tries to grab and confiscate this translation out of the hands of God's servants. It attempts to replace the spiritual translation of meaning into a secular way of thinking. It holds irrelevant the moral imperative to "care for one another as Christ cares for us" by redefining moral choices through the lens of self-interest, utilitarianism, hedonism, materialism, power, greed, and short-lived fame.

Throughout the history of the church, difficult times have required a caring translation of faith and action. Each generation has to define itself in light of the direction of the Holy Spirit. The adaptation of teaching and tradition are building blocks for the transmission of God's new creation of love and peace. The stresses of our modern culture require a caring focus on the primary purpose of the church, our calling, and direction. We are still on that journey from Emmaus back to Jerusalem. We still need to hear His voice explain the Scriptures to us and open our hearts to the power of the resurrection and live in the new creation. We are on the same walk of faith that the disciples have taken. You and I are called into the heart of Christ's love and to make Him known to others.

> We find no perfect place, no garden unbowed.
> No pleasure without another expectation,
> setting the bar of activities high-wired and proud,
> yet wondering in the tumbleweeds of limitations.

CHAPTER 6

The King of the New Creation

If we are to care and love one another as Christ cares for us, what is the character of Christ's teaching and action? We are told in the Scriptures that Jesus taught with authority, which was very different from the Pharisees. I don't think it meant that he was louder or more demanding or more charismatic. Over and over again in the Gospels, we see him at loggerheads with the religious authority. The thing that jumps out from this conflict is that Jesus is not afraid. He does not hide to avoid conflict, nor does He summon His supporters to defend Him. He stands His moral ground and doesn't back down by spinning the message to be more agreeable. He only speaks for His Father (John 8:27–30). He takes every opportunity given to Him, even speaking in His hometown, knowing that His message would not be well received.

Jesus doesn't couch His speech to accommodate the powerful. When He speaks, He says what He hears the Father saying. His authority comes from telling the truth. It comes from the risks He is willing to take. It comes from the works that He does. The authority of Jesus is an open invitation to follow Him (Jn. 5:16–23).

Jesus preached the kingdom of God as a starting point for His ministry. Every kingdom requires a king. The question that Pilate asks him at His trial is "Are you a king?" (John 18:37). The significance of this question can easily be overlooked. In executing Jesus, he is doing what the state does to all captured kings. It kills them and makes a spectacle of them. It treats them as a common criminal. This makes it easier to subject the followers. When Jesus replies, "You say so" (Matt. 27:11), He is acknowledging to Pilate that He is being treated like one, unlike an earthly king who rubs out the competition, even within his own family if necessary. Jesus's claim is to a kingdom of the heart. Pilate will order His execution because he does not recognize the difference. There is a whole set of grace principles at work with the kind of kingdom that Jesus offers.

The rule of law, science, and culture is subject to the new kingdom, the new creation of the heart. Kingdoms and kings come and go. Empires rise and fall, but the kingdom of the heart is never overcome. It cannot be defeated or ignored. Like many people, Pilate preferred the rule of the state and its culture to the kingdom of grace. The moral theology of choice and decision is predicated on the ground floor of the "Son of Man" who is its king and who brings the new creation with Him. If we're going to examine the nature of moral and ethical decisions, we need to start with the King. We will hold up His choices as a priori to the choices we make. Jesus and his caring for us is the mirror for our decisions. If we choose to live in the kingdom of grace, the guiding principles are tied to the person of Jesus Christ and the new creation.

The Beatitudes describe the character of the new creation. Jesus says, for example, "Blessed are the meek," which is a description of both the character of the King and disciples in His Kingdom (Matt. 5:1–13). Each "Blessed are" refers us back to the King who presides within the choices of those values congruent with His life and His choices. We begin to see a pattern emerge. "Love one another as I have loved you" is fleshed out by His teaching of the Beatitudes. To care means to be meek, to be a peacemaker, to be poor in spirit, and to be persecuted for the sake of the Gospel.

The biblical narrative does not address the complexity of all the moral choices we have to make today. However, the guidance we find in the Scriptures and in the Spirit will lead us into all truth (John 16:12–15). The Holy Spirit will maintain a faithful witness to what it means for the disciple to "love one another as Christ loves us." The condition of a person's conscience "held" within this framework will choose, by the activity of God's grace, to exercise the values and decisions congruent with God's love and purposes. Another way to say this theologically is a person's desire and commitment to do God's will (Garrigou-Lagrange, 1948).

Doing the will of God is a highly charged idea. Many people of various religions believe that they have an inside track as to what is God's will. A Muslim terrorist thinks, for example, that he is doing the will of Allah by strapping on a vest full of explosives to kill the infidels. They justify this terrible thing by citing the Koran and doing this for Allah's sake. Our country can see how barbaric and violent their acts are. We wonder how such people could even exist. Yet many in our society ignore the fifty million abortions in the United States that are caused by burning with saline, dismemberment, and brutality against unborn children, all of which the liberal culture supports. Is there an equivalency here when our courts make this kind of sin a right and the law of the land? Is there any way we can claim moral authority when sixty million possible citizens are not here, exterminated for no crime, and punished for existing? How is it possible that our society has so incinerated our values and freedoms and corrupted our land? No wonder that the moral aftershocks of these atrocities have led to a compulsive darkening of our consciences with drugs and alcohol. The effects on the nuclear family of this darkness are fueling the fetal demise of sanity and sobriety in our land. *Statistics from the National Right to Life, NRLC, abortions since 1973).*

Jesus invites us into a new universe, one that cares and suffers if necessary. It values the dignity of the person. The Scriptures introduce us into a counter-cultural, *new creation* that rests on the significance of the person's free will to act and choose the path of faith in Jesus Christ and faith in the Father's new creation.

> Praise God for the gift of our emancipation!
> The fertile soil of Christ's Harvest of Redemption,
> pregnant with the glorious gift of His salvation.
> Not alone with feigned regret, "Now the new creation!"

CHAPTER 7

Experiencing the New Creation

Sound moral decisions are grounded in an awareness that through grace, we are a new creation in Christ. There is a Christian way to appreciate and protect the environment. The beauty of the world and its incredible design leads to the Divine Artist who paints with matter, space, and energy. He signs His work with His name forever and is in everything. We don't have to somehow make creation fit our limitations. Humanity does not need to focus its creativity and discoveries by hoarding its resources. It can open up the folds of creation in Christ and discover the immense limitless fabric that is laid before us to love, respect, and enjoy.

Many today see our world as a pie with limited potential that we should be guilty about eating, since indulging ourselves on such a limited dessert makes it less available to others. Indeed, what is needed is a strict diet of self-reproach for needing anything from the mother's milk of our planet. This fatalistic view subjects us all to a "god" who is far too small. Nothing, it seems, will awaken this earthly god from the slumber of low expectations. It is such a shallow force and a lower power that has mistakenly abandoned so many people. It causes people to often destroy what little they have and desire to steal any leftovers from each other through economic strife and manipulation.

Jesus is the Lord. He has established a new creation. He is not anxious about provision. He takes five loaves and two fish and feeds five thousand men and woman (John 6:1–15). He fills the boat with fish telling them where to lay out their nets (Luke 5:1–11). Our Savior is not limited by our human fear of a deficient creator who is not quite up to the task without our help. Jesus is not fearful of the daily grind of want and insufficiency. Jesus is making all things new. He begins with creation itself. He confronts the idea that our narrow sight somehow describes the universe. He is in it all and for us all. What is required is trust in the Father and in His Son so that creation itself will be opened up to us by His Holy Spirit. He confronts the mythic gods of want and insufficient supply with the new creation of His Father's generosity and abundance. The new creation is accessed only through Jesus Christ: He is the way, the truth, and the life (John 6:35–40). He is the new Adam that has inherited everything, and much more than that—He brings all things into one. He is the alpha and the omega, the beginning and the end (Rev. 1:8). In Jesus, all the opposites come together in unity and merge into light: "And I have given them the glory you gave me, so that they may be one, as we are one, I in them and you in me, that they may be brought to perfection as one, that the world may know that you sent me, and that you loved them even as you loved me" (John 17:22–24). The benevolent grace of the new creation is now available to those who believe in Him. (Col. 1:15–20).

The Sacraments, the Word, and Portals into the New Creation

We celebrate the Holy Eucharist on Sundays, and we go to communion. Here we receive the Word of God and the sacrament of the body and blood of Christ. This would be pointless, if not for the new creation that Jesus has provided for us through the Holy Spirit. The priest or minister and the community offer and pray over the gifts of bread and wine, asking the Holy Spirit to make them the body and blood of Christ. When we receive them in faith, we receive the new creation into our body and soul. How can these elements change into something more through prayer? It's not humanly possible, but in the new creation, it is the true nature of things. Since all these things are possible only in Christ through the Spirit, we enter into the territory of the new creation where God supplies, feeds, and gives all the grace needed for His Word to bring forth life. He affirms us in it, that is why in John's Gospel, it's described as abiding in Him. Abiding means being in the new creation (John 15:1–17). Jesus provides much more than bread and fish or wine—He provides Himself, which includes all things that are one in Him (John 17:6–16). The universe and everything in it belong to the new creation, and so do we. Putting out our hands and receiving the *bread of life*, we commune with the substance of redemption, love, and the liberated pattern of our freedom in Christ. We receive Him, and we receive the new creation into our hearts forever. We are consecrated in it and made holy, pure, and precious to God (1 Peter 2:9–10 and John 17:1–26).

The *sacrament of baptism* is our emancipation from death into life. It's a leap into the gift of the new creation. The baptism that Jesus is baptized into, through His death and resurrection, funnels us through our baptism into a new pattern of life. We leave behind the old man, as Paul says, and we are born again into the kingdom of love and light (2 Cor. 5:16–21). Death is put behind us, and freedom is open to us. Sin dies in us, and grace and love are sown in our hearts. We become children of God and children of the new creation (Rom. 8:14–17).

Baptism is a singular pivot point. When we look inward, we don't just have a solitary experience of our thoughts, feelings, and attitudes (Savage, 1996). We experience Jesus in our Spirit (Rom. 8:16), "the Son of Man and the Son of God" who lives in us. He leads us into His heart and by the Holy Spirit into the new creation so that we can experience it with Him. Baptism is a plunge into the ocean of Christ's redemption and into His Father's new creation.

Many people think that once a person is baptized, they've punched their ticket into heaven. Church is optional; at best it's an occasional duty. The expectations of church participation burdens their weak faith, since churches are not much different from their dysfunctional families. They see Christianity being dismissed, often ridiculed, and blamed for society's problems by the culture. The secular worldview infects today's society with a deadly pessimism. Baptism does far more than produce a kind of religious credit card. Our baptism is the gift of God's life in us. It changes everything.

There is a common, cultural, unconscious premise that humanity can manufacture and fashion creation for its own ends. Once our society believes that it can manipulate creation by and for itself, who needs God? The truth is, the more we try to put creation into the box, based on our limited understanding, the more things get twisted by our pride and arrogance. The book of Genesis tells us about this self-delusion, from the expulsion from the garden to the Tower of Babel. It warns us of the confusion that comes with overstepping our limits and the consequences of our hubris. Baptism into the body of Christ acknowledges that the new creation is ushered in on God's terms. It grafts us into the vine of the Father's worldview of redemption in Jesus and into the new wine of the Holy Spirit (Jn. 15:1–9).

Water is a symbol of the new creation in Jesus. We acknowledge its mystery, its power, and its connection to serve God's purposes. Out of the waters of creation God brought forth a teeming variety of life (Gen. 1:20). Through our baptism, He regenerates the new life of grace in us and blesses us with the abundance of His new creation. Accepting Jesus as your Lord and Savior will do that to you. It provokes us to live, in the Spirit, the values of Christ's commandment, "To love one another as He loves us" (John 13:34).

I remember that when I was baptized in the Spirit, for about a week everything seemed brighter and filled with color. I felt more alive and aware of God's presence in all things. It was like some spiritual endorphin's were released. The more I prayed, both in the Spirit and in my own words, the more I experienced the world in a new way. Many people I have interviewed recount a similar thing happening to them. It was, I think, a spiritual awakening to the new creation. I sometimes wish that I could feel that same conversion again. Jesus reminds me to hold fast to the faith I have received. I don't need to conjure up an old memory. Jesus is producing more and more grace for me through His redemption. My relationship with Him is more than enough, and so is His new creation in me and you.

The *sacrament of marriage* is the yoking together of two very different persons choosing to be one in Christ Jesus. The sacrament is not a witness to sameness but a witness to the new creation. God brings about the union of many differences into one flesh. A man and a woman are different sexually, emotionally, and psychologically. The new creation is about establishing unity in these differences as God makes us one. Out of the intimacy of love and the coming together in unity—"marriage"—produces a child, and a new creation, is brought into the world. A collaboration of God's creation and our participation is born. Is every child conceived by loving parents or in loving ways? We know that sadly, this is not the case. Still, God's plan in giving life, revealed in Christ's life, death, and resurrection is to gather us into a new creation. It means something and reveals something about His plan for all humanity. "Life is difficult," as Scott Peck says in his book *The Road Less Traveled*. No matter how painful it may be or abrasive or how much suffering may arrive, God and His new creation, through the resurrection in the power of the Holy Spirit, will break through (Phil. 2:6–11).

If we value marriage as a portal of grace into the new creation, we will also uphold the value of life. As the meaning of marriage has been degraded and marginalized and even its definition changed, so has the value of human life been devalued and degraded. Who would have ever thought before *Roe v. Wade* that our American Constitution would be used to justify the elimination of our future, promoted as a means to justify an attack on the foundation of a civil society? No future citizen is safe, and the family is teetering on the edge of irrelevancy. Divorce has become almost as common as marriages, according to the *Center for Disease Control, CDC (2018) statistics that report 6.5 marriages per 1000 in contrast to 2.9 divorces per 1000.*

Our cultural deity has decided, for our own good, that marriage is whatever you want it to be if it's "loving." The worship of sexual gratification is the culture's new sacrament. It immerses a person into meaninglessness and moral confusion. The resultant response is to anesthetize this defeat with compulsive acting out. This cycle is repeated over and over again until the person dies morally at their own hand. The fixation on death is gaining ground partly because human life has become subject to a weak immoral nondefense. Just watch how many times the program *The Walking Dead* is promoted on television. It's a program title that perfectly describes our cultural and moral decline. The real sacrament of marriage is the only antidote to this conflict. It's the sacrament most under assault because it's the most important witness to love in the world. The gift of Christian marriage brings hope to the world. It contrasts the empty promises of the culture, where nothing lasts, where there is no safety, where the family is just a cluster of confused relationships(John Paul II, 1995).

St. Paul points out to us that we no longer are to live as slaves to sin and death, but to live in the Spirit (Rom. 8:1–13). He contrasts the pagan worldview of his day to the Gospel of freedom of the people of God. He's pointing out a similar conflict that we have today. Our media and the cultural elite have a vendetta against the family, because it's the place where we give the greatest witness to Jesus with our spouses, children, relatives, and friends. Jesus welcomes the gift of marriage as a testimony of God's new creation. He is the Bridegroom, and we are His bride, the church (Rev. 21:1–5). He brings in that day of the new creation with all its, glory, love, and Spirit. Jesus is here again *"realized eschatology"* and He brings the new creation with Him (Brown, et al. 1968).

The *sacrament of reconciliation* draws us into the heart of Christ's purpose of redemption. Jesus's words of forgiveness in His teaching, and from the cross, coupled with its extension to the church, transfer us from sin back into harmony with Christ and the new creation. We are questioned in the Scriptures how can we say, "We love the God we can't see and at the same time hate the brother or sister that we can see"? (1 John 5:20). Forgiveness intersects us with the Father's purposes through Christ's incarnation. He came to set us free from sin and death and to make us God's children. The sacrament of reconciliation will draw those who use it straight into the meaning of God's plan for their life. Connecting us back into communion with Jesus reestablishes us into the heart of God's care. We experience a vital gift of His new creation.

Reconciliation is when I acknowledge my sin, ask for forgiveness from God and the person or persons I have offended, and give and receive absolution. I discover the depth of God's mercy. Recognizing my weakness takes nothing away from me. Shame and guilt are not necessarily the product of honest self-evaluation but are often the result of painful avoidance and secret motives. That's why the sacrament is so vital for our reclamation. Both parties discover the gift of receiving and giving absolution. The primary purpose of Christ's gift of redemption is this ministry of bringing peace to our brokenness. We discover what it means to live in the grace of giving and receiving forgiveness from one another. One of the essential characteristics, therefore, of living in the new creation is being in the milieu of reconciliation.

Choosing to live with the values of our broken world, apart from exercising the gift of repentance and forgiveness, is to validate the slavery of our fallen nature and its twisted worldview. When Jesus says that "apart from me you can do nothing" (John 15:5–10), that is what He means. The new creation will not respond to our demands for its fragmentation. Human maneuvering, manipulation, and sin only drive the wedge deeper into the bedrock of humanity's higher moral calling. Sin polarizes and distorts the essential ingredients needed to build unity, love, and faithfulness. Without this safety, the world is a dangerous place.

Paul says it this way in 2 Corinthians 5:12–21, "that we are ambassadors of reconciliation, Christ making His appeal through us." An ambassador speaks with the authority of the king or ruler, but the ambassador also identifies with what is in the best interest of the country he/she represents. Jesus is the king, but we also appeal for that new country. The new creation is our homeland. That's why in John's Gospel, He speaks to us in chapters 15, 16, and 17 of a relationship with us that is entwined in unity like a vine to its branches. It calls us to abide in a deep fellowship that is united in purpose, love, and faithfulness. Jesus lays down his life willingly to birth and bring forth into being the Father's new creation. No one takes His life from Him. He willingly lays it down (John 9:17–19). Jesus's suffering is like a woman who struggles in childbirth, risking even her life to bring into the world a child, a new creation (John 16:20–23). So Jesus lays down His life through His suffering on the cross, bringing forth life to all people who believe, making them new. We are God's children, and all creation receives this benefit too. The sacrament of reconciliation is an essential ingredient for our walk with God. If we know how much we are forgiven, we appreciate how much we are loved (Luke 7:36–50). We live by grace in our homeland of the new creation. Holiness is conscientiously maintaining our bond to Jesus Christ, through living by grace in the Spirit, and experiencing the Father's new creation, not only someday after we die, but right now!

If we focus on the material breach of the law, Paul says, we are convicted of our sins. Indeed, the only thing that we can be sure of is that we are under the taskmaster of the law's demands and its judgments (Rom. 7:1–25). We cannot wish away or disown our condition. Our abject poverty is our need for emancipation from sin and death. It's only human folly and delusion to think or believe we can change the situation on our own. From where we stand, it's impossible to break the hold of sin, its effects, and its resultant guilt and shame. Denial will push us into more compulsive misbehavior, fear, and pain.

Romans 8 introduces us into that new country of liberation and freedom. Jesus through His death and resurrection created for all of us a place in God's heart. The good standing, we have in Christ, through His redemption, releases us from the law of sin and death to live in the same "Spirit that Raised Christ from the dead" (Rom. 8:9–12). What changes a person is not the law Paul points out but the benefits of grace and redemption.

The sacrament of reconciliation is not an attempt to edify ourselves or keep God's judgment at bay. It's not a tool for self-reproach or even self-judgment. It's not the work of the church to expiate our tethered guilt or shame. It offers reconciliation as a joyful participation in giving and receiving mercy, love, and renewal. It opens the door for us to walk into our homeland, the country of our redemption and the freedom to be God's children, to be heirs to the kingdom, heirs to the new creation.

Ordination and Confirmation, Ministering the New Creation

I place these sacraments together. They make concrete the ministry of Christ to care for one another. There is no greater gift than caring for one another as Jesus cares for us. We move into a common purpose and life with Christ through self-donation and service. The gift of grace and the movement of the Holy Spirit provided the power to direct the apostles forward into Pentecost (Acts 2:1–13). Jesus instructed them to wait for this event to occur. He sent the Spirit that hovered over the first creation and brought forth the cosmos and all life into the universe, to baptize them into His new creation and send them out to the world.

Tongues of fire came upon them and enkindled their hearts with this new reality. Suddenly, they could speak God's Word with courage. They could sing a new song with the language of the angelic hosts. God's glory filled the temple that was inside them with praise and adorned them with His mighty power. Ministry is what every Christian is graced into though their baptism. We are empowered to live the life of the Spirit that confers the new creation into our hearts. Like the apostles, we are born again through this Holy Spirit into our new homeland; and like them, we are to invite others to experience this too.

Confirmation is an adult ascent into the heart of the Father's care. Through grace in the Spirit, the gifts are manifested for the building up of God's people (1 Cor. 12:1–19). The person affirms their baptism, often made for them when they were babies, to the people of God. Now aglow in the Spirit, Jesus sanctifies and brings them into His new creation, blessing them in His ministry of caring.

Everything that can be said about ordination can also be said about confirmation. Still, ordination to the deaconate or priesthood or episcopate has a unique refinement of this calling to serve God's people. Many books have been written on this subject. My purpose is to recognize that the focus of these two sacraments are "callings in the Spirit" to serve His people with God's heart of care. A pastor needs to believe in the person of Jesus and the new creation that Jesus reveals through His grace in the Spirit. Signs and wonders are produced when this belief takes root and grows like a mustard seed (Matt. 13:31–32). For the quality of ministry to mature, we need to get outside the cultural expectations that sometimes infect the church. We often float along in the tide of the institutional realities, saying mass, doing funerals, having weddings, conducting Bible studies, or participating in stewardship programs, keeping the lights on and the doors open. These are important needs to be sure. However, if church leadership focuses on these things, we may not venture out into the creative depths of Jesus's powerful resurrected life, where there is uncertainty and risk. It's often seen as a negative thing by many, especially church boards, when the Spirit begins to lead the church into a place of insecurity with new directions and opportunities. Instead, we tend to fall back on our old alignment with avoidance. The greatest hope we offer to others is what the culture tunes out. Few want to wait for "someday when we get to heaven," especially when it seems easier to believe that we can be better served by our dreams and fantasies of mythic-cultural rewards, an example would be the lottery. The church has to embrace anew what the apostles never forgot. We desire now to marry our hearts with Jesus and His cause of redemption. We live in the new creation with Him now. We are led by the Spirit through His love now. Waiting for permission from our own foolish resistance and insecurity will not produce fruit. The harvest will rot on the tree as long as our hope is stymied by doubt and fear. The church is at its best when it's contrasting the Gospel and its power and depth over and against the culture's shallow and empty promises. Ordained leadership in this contest is not a protective castle, hidden behind doors of religious pretense. It means to take the standard of grace and the new creation right up the hill of disbelief. We are to claim that victory of Christ over the world tainted by sin and death. Now, I can believe in that new world. I can endure with hope, trusting in Jesus and being led in the Spirit by God's grace. It's more than enough to carry the difficulties and trials of the day. Living in the new creation is our eternal prize.

I have been a priest for many years. I know that the church can be a hard environment to deal with. Every servant has to experience suffering with Jesus for the sake of the new creation. Love for God's people is purified by our willingness to enter the crucible of the community's failings and our own. Birthing the new creation with Christ is not without pain. It's not without sweat and tears (2 Cor. 6:1–10).

The story of the transfiguration (Mark 9:1–8) speaks to the reality of Christ as the Shepherd of the new creation. The Gospel places us in a scene of glory that envelops the three apostles. Biblical scholars think this is a post-resurrection story that Mark has placed in this part of His Gospel to advance his narrative and to show that Jesus is the Son of God. (Brown, et al., 1968). I think it's much more than that. It demonstrates for us the experience of the new creation that the leadership of the church would need to remember when they were suffering for their faith. Future leaders would need to know, in the Spirit, that the new creation is a reality. The law represented by Moses (Ex. 3:1–11) and the prophetic tradition represented by Elijah (1 Kings 18:1–39) are fulfilled and surpassed by Jesus and the new creation. The same voice of the Father that presided over His baptism by John speaks to them through the lens of glory and affirms Jesus. He is the Son of God and is to be trusted, listened to, and followed (Mk. 1:9–12). Ordained leadership means a commitment to enter the experience of accepting the sufferings of Christ and participating in being transformed by the Holy Spirit and living in the new creation.

The sacrament of anointing the sick, is a witness to the activity of Jesus and is one of the benefits of living in the Spirit of God's new creation. In baptism, there is part of the ritual where the person is anointed with oil, and they are marked as Christ's own forever (Book of Common Prayer, 1978), but in this sacrament, we ask for God to touch our sickness and pain with healing. The anointing oil represents the activation of the Spirit to bring healing and forgiveness to the person in need. It also is a transcendent link to Jesus's ministry. It opens us up to the new creation where there is a real solace for the person needing comfort, compassion, restoration, and healing.

Some priests or ministers withhold this sacrament because of a person's standing in the church or denomination. It's as if there is some kind of test required to receive the ministry of the church when a person needs the effects of the benefits won for us by Christ given in the new creation. There is no greater affront to Christ's ministry of caring and redemption than to withhold the sacrament of anointing because of church legal requirements and its own set of canonical scruples.

We are all going to transition through death into the fullness of the new creation. Jesus's redemption takes the sting of fear out of that journey (Rom. 8:1–3). Medical treatment can be a means for us to see that God partners with us in caring for our pain and sickness.

I have been a hospital chaplain for over thirty years, and I have been blessed to be present and praying for many people who are moving from this world into the new creation. I have even experienced that in my own life. My wife, Dorothy, died in March 2015 after a long illness with Parkinson's. My family and our church and I prayed for her healing every day. After the funeral several weeks later, as I was driving to church, I found myself feeling guilty like I failed her somehow. In spite of all my prayers, my efforts, and those of the doctors, I couldn't get her well. I couldn't protect her from death. I pulled off the road and parked the car and just wept. I cried out to Jesus in pain and sorrow, looking for answers why this had happened and how I had let her down. Then that voice of His spoke in my head and heart.

"Just stop it," He said, in a voice that was caring but also firm. "What more could I have done for her? I love her, I made her perfect, and I healed her and answered all your prayers and hers. I gave my life for her and filled her with the Holy Spirit and brought her into the abundance of the new creation. I made her transition painless and easy. What more could I have done?"

"Nothing more, my Lord, You did everything for her, all that she needed," I replied through my tears. "How can I live without her?"

He said, "I will be all you need."

I felt like Job who had been put in his place (Job, 38, 39 & 40). Not in a bad way, but in a firm and loving way. I look back at that prayer now as being an important breakthrough because God took the sting out of her loss. Do I still grieve her and miss her? Of course, I do. I know sometimes that when I anoint someone with oil they are receiving this sacrament of healing to enter the new creation forever. It's also true that sometimes Jesus wants to anoint us personally in prayer so that we might experience being transfigured by his grace in the Spirit just like the apostles (Mark 9:2–13).

> I look into the pool of love's tranquil oasis—
> reflecting the image that God has presented,
> with light, and shimmering incandescence,
> illuminating the Adam His Spirit resurrected.

Chapter 8

Experiencing the Word, Prayer, and Community

I place these three things, the Word, Prayer and Community together because they are so entwined with each other. They are a trinity of three characteristics that express a unity of one purpose to reveal the love of Jesus personally to the world. The Word, the Old and New Testament, brings us into a relationship with Christ; this didn't happen on its own. God's Word is written down with us and for us. It was redacted, edited, translated, and brought together through a process of historical growth (Brown, 1968). The Bible didn't fall out of the sky. It was first handed down in oral stories, told around the campfire, remembered, collected, and then written and refined. The Word is God's caring. It has been revealed through the faith experience of individuals and their communities. In this way, the Bible is just like all of us. We come into this world the same way. We make our mark in society. We learn and grow through our history. Our experiences shape and refine our choices. We, like the Scriptures, tell our story through our history, memories, and background. These three portals into the new creation point us to the "perfecter of our faith." Like any organism, there is a unifying purpose. Our bodies are interconnected and maintained by the unity of all the parts functioning together. The harmony of our complex chemical and biological systems provokes the response of awe and wonder, the more science discovers. Our creation is not an accident but a well-orchestrated symphony of delicate and intricate details. Nature itself calls out for us to recognize the grand composer who wrote the music. We were created not to fear this universe or its songsmith, but to dance and clap our hands. Sin stole away God's melody, but Jesus has brought the music back into our hearts. Now in Him, and through His death and resurrection, we can sing again the song of the new creation. St. Paul says it this way, "We are the Body of Christ" (1 Cor. 13:27). The Word of God in the Scriptures introduces us into the spiritual meaning of the Father's will. The Word instructs us and invites us into the new creation. The abundance of God's love, forgiveness, and grace causes us to celebrate our liberation in the Spirit. It's the antithesis of the culture's false gods and its fixation on death and destruction. Paul indicates that living in the Spirit frees us from sin and renews our minds and hearts to live by faith into God's new world. We are meant not to live by the flesh but to live in the Spirit (Rom. 7:4–7). The result of this life with God the Father through Jesus places us in the orbit of the new creation. The newness we receive as His Body is not a static thing, based on our limited understanding of our material world. It's rather a revelation of the Father's reality that includes the vastness and beauty of all creation. The "body of Christ" isn't a limitation to our anatomy. It blesses it. We are spiritually grafted together through community in mirroring Christ's glory (Rom. 5:12–20). The Word leads us into a deeper experience of the new creation that we are meant to share together. "Being in Christ, a new creation," identifies us with the community of faithful witnesses that worship the one who saved us from the laws futility and the constraints of limited materiality and mortality (Rev. 22:1–5).

The importance of community seems to be the hardest concept for us to grasp. The new creation is not a solitary experience. The person who loves others with the love of Jesus enters into it. I realize that this can be the hardest part of walking with Jesus. It's the easiest thing in the world to blame others when we face hardships. Most of the time it's because of family, friends, or other community relationships. Few people today look at community as a strength. It's often seen as something we struggle with, try to endure, or avoid, because it's the place where there's great joy or, more often, great pain. That's why God the Father wants us to learn from it. If you asked a hundred people to express what they're looking for in a church, my guess is that there would be a hundred different answers. We want something like the church we remember as children. We want a church, and a family, where the pastor is friendly and outgoing. We want a church that's stable and not angry. We know we want something, and we have an idea what it is and what it's not. We unconsciously look for a kind of utopian community that will meet our needs. We want what is not possible through our own creation. When it falls short of our fantasy, many drop out or get angry or just stay and make others miserable. We can do to the church what the culture and its false gods do to us. We build judgments or make excuses or just give up trying. We fail to see that in Christ Jesus, we are meant to live in and experience the new creation (Gal. 5:13–26).

Since my wife died of Parkinson's, I've noticed that my prayer life has changed. Sometimes I feel such a deep loss that words cannot convey its meaning. I believe that what has happened to her is glorious. Yet I am left with such a groaning sorrow at times that I have nothing to say to God except "Jesus." It's usually mixed with tears. I have discovered something in this that has shown me the Father's love in a way that's hard to describe. When I align my pain and loss with His, on the cross for me and others, I have an *abba* experience and deeply relate to Him through it. I pray the name of Jesus now differently than before. My prayer was often about what I needed or for my friends or about my struggles. Since Dorothy's transformation to eternal life, when I say the name of Jesus, I feel His sufferings and love for me and the world. It's not an empty pain, bereft of meaning, or a hopeless acknowledgment to the nature of our fallen world. Rather, a new reality has taken root in my soul that propels me to hope and trust in Him (Rom. 8:14–17).

Living in the new creation is about stepping into our future each day. It means that we grow into our new life of freedom from sin. Growth in prayer is an acknowledgment that we are also growing into the Father's eternal country—the one planted in our hearts in baptism and now flowering into the new creation, recognizing that we are reborn and that we live a new life. No human power can give this gift. No one can conjure it up or pretend it's theirs without Christ. No one can buy it or steal it or carry it away. The world of the broken promises of sin will try to imitate it with money, power, or pleasure. It will never measure up because it will not last. We discover in the Word made flesh the amazing quality of God's love for His people and indeed for all creation and we groan for it (Rom. 8:22–24).

In the Our Father, we say, "Thy kingdom come" (Matt. 6:10). We are not just praying for the return of Christ but His kingdom. The new creation is another way of saying and acknowledging this invitation. It's not meant to be a faraway event, someday. It's the coming of His new creation in us in the Spirit and offering us to the Father through Christ's redemption. It's a "now" event full of infinite possibilities in Jesus that makes "all things new." Praying in the Spirit is a recognition of this new creation. God's grace pours out the Spirit's character of praise and worship (Rom. 8:26–30). It's like a breath of fresh air to our soul. Praying in this way connects us to that day when languages and cultures will not keep God's people apart. It's a release from the constraint of sin's ego-centered miscommunication with God and each other. The new Adam has overcome the world with love, hope, and faith. Worshiping God in the Spirit affirms the Father's initial design of establishing a universal language of prayer and worship. Prayer in the Spirit ministers to us by saturating us in the "living water" of the new creation (John 4:13–15).

Prayer in this paradigm is opposed to the faithless fatalism that doubts God's Word that our culture preaches as its gospel. Prayer in the new creation is a belief that the Father provides what is needed. It trusts in the power of God's love to overcome evil and sin. It hopes in the transformation of the world into the new creation of unity and peace. Prayer in the Spirit is to walk with Jesus in the new eternal garden, worshiping the Father in Spirit and truth.

Prayer does not just lead us to an inner dialogue—it also leads me to you. Community carries prayer into my experience of being with others. It ties us to family and to a common life together. Jesus had a community around Him because He lived in the new creation in the Spirit, and it led Him into the experience of others. Throughout the Gospels, He ministers, cares, loves, touches, teaches, heals, and builds a community wherever He goes. We see Him in communion with the Father in His prayer and with His friends. He is a man of community (Jn. 17:1–25).

Prayer that leads us to self-preoccupation is not prayer. It's often just self-delusion.

Our culture places its highest importance on our ego needs. Catering to the ego sells products. You will be loved, sexy, and noticed if you buy this car, use this bank, get this outfit, or wear this perfume. Chasing after our needs leads to isolation and wounds our sense of community. Once we step out of community, we step out of the benefit of living in the new creation. The greatest folly of making culture divine is the isolation it causes. I'm not talking about the absence of communication, but the never-ceasing intrusion of this new electronic deity. Hurtful things can be said without thinking. Texting, for example, has caused the nature of relationships to be lost in the immediacy of shallow and distant attempts at bonding. It's the saddest commentary of our times that so many people have little regard for the feelings of others, never questioning their own motives and agendas. The immediacy of the moment is the thing that matters, and since it's instantaneous, it must be right. Our computer culture promotes the use of these kinds of tools to replace face-to-face communication. It is often more difficult to conduct business, resolve issues, and develop lasting relationships when the tools we use are limited by our narrow perceptions. It is a kind of built-in confusion that leads to a one-sided interpretation of events that can stifle our ability to get a broader understanding of the facts and a more holistic appreciation of other points of view, along with, leading to isolation, and depression. (*Computers/impact, 2020*).

> I hear the gurgling, bubbling, sloshing sounds,
> of water, rivulets, birthing an ocean of crescendos.
> A tidal force that crashes, retreats, and rebounds,
> with ancient percussion's, vibrations, and echoes.

CHAPTER 9

Three Characteristics of the New Creation

Divine Providence is one of the key elements of being in harmony with God the Father's plans and purposes. If we are living in the new creation, we are being where, and doing what, He wants us to do. A person living in the new creation gets moved around by the Holy Spirit. I have experienced God's guidance in my ministry. Jesus seems to set me up with divine appointments. It's an exciting adventure and blessing to trust in the Father's providence and to see His influence and guidance in my life (Acts, 8:26–40).

After Dorothy and I were married, we maintained our belief that I was still called to be a priest. We had begun to attend an Episcopal church. I had spoken to the rector about my intention to serve God's people. We had no money; and going back to the seminary for a year of further studies, which was required, seemed impossible. My parish decided to send me for an interview to see the school and make some contacts. I visited Seminary of the Southwest, which is in Austin, Texas. They told me about the cost of tuition, student housing, and the money I would need just to meet basic expenses. I came back home feeling pretty defeated. Dorothy just said, "We'll just have to pray for a miracle." So we did. She said, "Let's make a novena to the Sacred Heart." Now I must say that I never liked this kind of prayer. Saying the same prayers for nine days seemed like magical thinking to me. After all, I'm a well-rehearsed charismatic prayer machine. I thought, okay, what harm would it do? Maybe something would happen, if it was God's will. Somehow I managed to put my resistance aside, and we completed praying the novena. Nothing happened. We just continued living in our little apartment. A couple of weeks later, Dorothy's boss was coming back to Phoenix, and she needed someone to pick her up at the airport. I volunteered, with Dot's encouragement, and went to the airport to meet her. It was early summer, and it was hot and busy with a lot of people all in a hurry. I walked up a long ramp to get to the gate as her flight was arriving. I heard my name being called up ahead of me. I recognized Bishop Joseph Harte, the retired Episcopal bishop, waving at me. He came over to me, and the first thing he said in his resonant booming voice was "Michael, would you still like to go to the seminary?"

I replied, "Yes, I would, Bishop."

He grinned and put his hand on my shoulder and said, "Well, I think I have some good news for you. I have just been given a $5,000 grant, and my friend, the retired presiding bishop Heinz, has also been given a $5,000 grant. I'm going to recommend that he and I should give it to Seminary of the Southwest for you. I will get the ball rolling, call the seminary next week, and you should be able to start school in the fall."

I couldn't believe it. I stammered, "Yes, I'll do that. Thank you, Bishop."

He shook my hand and said, "Great! I've got to go. See you later."

With that said, he turned and briskly walked away. Just then my wife's boss found me, and after a hug, on we went. When I got home, I broke the news to Dorothy. We were very excited and giddy about this miracle. The next week I got a call from the seminary saying that I had received a one-year grant to go to school there.

I asked, "How can my family and I find a place to live? Is there housing on the campus available?"

"There is foreign student housing, but that's for folks from overseas," the secretary replied, with a charming, soft Southern Texas drawl.

She continued, "But seeing that y'all are from Arizona, you just might qualify. I'll call you back and let you know if something can be worked out."

She was good to her word and called me a couple of hours later and said, "I checked with the dean. He said it's okay for you and your family to live on campus. It so happens that we have a two-bedroom apartment on the first floor. It's pretty spacious and would fit you, folks. There is one problem though."

I felt my enthusiasm suddenly checked. "What's that?"

"The dean told me that you would need to take clinical pastoral education this summer."

"How do I get that class?"

"Well," she replied, "you have to register and be accepted into a program. It's too late to do that. Classes are about to start in a week or so. But you know, I heard that they might have an opening at Austin State Hospital. I could give you their number, and you could call over there and see."

I felt a glimmer of hope break through. "Please give me that number, and I'll call them right away."

When I called over to the chaplain's office, the secretary confirmed that they had an opening. They wanted me to submit some paperwork, and in a couple of days, I was in. The whirlwind was not over. There were a million details to attend to. They all easily fell into place. We stored some items and managed to stuff the necessities for two adults and two children into a little trailer hitched to the back of our two-door VW Rabbit. We headed down the road to our future a few days later. After three long days on the road, we arrived late in the afternoon at the seminary. We checked in at the administration office and got the keys. We found our apartment to be very nice and tastefully furnished.

Dorothy went back to the office a little later and asked the lady at the desk if there were any job openings at the seminary.

She answered, "Not at this time, but I heard that they might be looking for a secretary at All Saints. I could give you the number, and you could call them. They might still be there."

"Oh yes," Dorothy excitedly replied. "Thank you very much."

She immediately called the church. The rector answered and hired her just talking to her over the phone. She started work the next day.

We found out later that the grants that we received had been given to Bishop Heinz and Bishop Harte by someone from that parish.

I'm sharing this story to show that when we are in the new creation, we are also living in the Father's holy will. The reverse is also true: if we are living in the Father's holy will, we are living in the new creation. The novena we said wasn't to make God the Father respond to our needs. It was for us to open our hearts and to trust Him with them. Like that initial drive we made in the desert I referred to before, we had to believe in the Father's Word without seeing.

Looking at the ministry of Jesus Christ, we can appreciate how He is moved by His Father's hand. His birth is providential. His ministry is providential. It begins by hearing the Father's voice affirm Him, then being led by the Spirit into the wilderness (Matt. 4:1–11). He moved from town to town, as He healed the sick and released people from the bondage of evil, sickness, and death.(Jn. 11:38–44). Jesus lives in the new creation all the time, since He is Lord, and always follows the Father's will. Everywhere He brings the new creation with Him. There is no death, brokenness, slavery to sin, and sickness or demonic oppression in this new creation. He says, "He has overcome the world, and not to be afraid" (Jn. 16:33). He's revealing to us the new creation by being obedient to the Father's plan of salvation. Jesus takes the place of the broken, fragmented world tied to disobedience and sin and redeems it with His Father's love by shedding His blood. Following Jesus means living into His Father's new reality and trusting and believing in it too. In John's Gospel, Jesus tells us that He is doing what he sees His Father doing. What is His work? It's to bring the new creation to us through the Holy Spirit now! When we are living in it, we see the works of God. We see miracles, because in the new creation, we are holy in Christ. We move in the pattern of the Father's salvation in Jesus, and we share the Good News that Jesus has set us free from sin and death and transferred us into the new creation. Heaven is not a final resting place, but a dynamic experience of living in the new creation now and forever. We get to taste it in advance (Acts 3:1–10).

When I was a little kid, I used to get my parents to give me dessert first, as long as I promised to eat the rest of my food. Of course, in my mind, this never included eating peas. Even today, now and then, I will eat my dessert first. Somehow it makes the dessert that much sweeter.

Jesus initiates us into the life of God the Father's providence so that we can taste our dessert first and hunger all the more for the prize.

We see in the Scriptures how Jesus introduces the apostles into the experience of trusting in Him. The first thing we notice is that they followed Him. Jesus set the direction, timing, and movements for each day because He followed the Father's plan (Eph. 1:3–13). Believing in the message of Jesus meant following where He led. Jesus tells them that "He is the way, the truth, and the life." He's gently moving the apostles forward, a little at a time, into the journey of belief by trusting His Father's words and works (John 7:24–27).

When I go swimming, I don't just jump into the water. I want to know if it's really cold. I might get such a shock that swimming would be very unpleasant. Just staying in the water might be a challenge. I slowly enter the pool, taking time to get used to the different temperature. Once I'm all in, and I'm adjusted to the water, it's a lot easier to swim and spend time enjoying the experience. Trusting in God's providence is a bit like adapting to the water temperature. We see, throughout the Bible, that the Father's calling on a person's life means to trust Him. We are drawn into this way of life, a little at a time. Sometimes the experience of meeting Jesus can be an instantaneous transformation like St. Paul (Acts:9:1–13), yet even Paul took three years to be prepared for his ministry. He had to discover what it meant to evangelize people, even the pagans. He needed to learn the art of following and trusting Jesus in the Spirit. Paul learned to trust in the Father's provision. He discovered the "works" of the new creation: "It's not by bread alone, or by the will of man, but by every Word that comes from the mouth of God" (Luke 4:4). Placing trust in the created universe only leads to fragmentation and disappointment. Trusting in Jesus opens the new creation up to us in the Spirit and makes "all things possible for those who have faith" (Mk. 9:23). When God created Adam and Eve, He placed them in the garden. They enjoyed the provident care of God the Father without any worry, sweat, or toil (Gen. 1:27–28). The material universe was theirs to enjoy without the constraint of distrust, fear, or loss. You and I step back onto that stage of belonging in harmony with nature, through the grace of Christ's death and resurrection in the Spirit. Jesus was not the only one raised from death. All things were brought back into harmony and communion with the Father's intention of creating all things "good." Jesus provides that spark of holiness that ignites our hearts and the universe into a "Living Flame of Love" (St. John of the Cross, 1991 edition). Anyone who follows Him is a new creation.

We draw sustenance and solace from the Word of God that describes the characteristics of the Father's personal revelation. It's not enough for Him to stand outside the ring and heckle the participants or even to referee the combatants. The Father's engagement with us and creation provokes His plan to enter the ring Himself, and He invites us to join Him. Jesus knows the price. He trusts the intention of the Father's purpose of redemption. He is willing to trust that the fight He must wage is not against us, but for us. He enters the ring to take the blows, of sin, the enemy, lies, fear, sickness, and death, and lays down His life. When the bell rings, the Father's glory is left standing. The new creation rises from the canvas of the world's lost values; and we, those who believe, rise with it.

Reconciliation within the framework of the new creation is a reclamation of our birthright as God's children through Christ's redemption. Forgiveness of sin not only puts us back into harmony with God the Father through Jesus Christ in the Spirit, but also opens to us the new creation. Sin entangles us into a fallen universe affected by the worldview of loss, death, sickness, pain, fear, sin, and broken dreams. The disciple who chooses Jesus Christ, and desires to live in His Word, will become vibrant and born again. Being reconciled to Christ and one another matches up our "desires" with the loving experience of God's purposes. The Father's worldview is Jesus Christ. His power to accomplish its singularity is the dynamic gift of the Holy Spirit. It's inevitable that God will bring about His plan. He will make "all things into unity in Christ Jesus" (Eph. 1:9–11). Until that day of completion arrives when the universe and the "Alpha and the Omega meet" (Rev. 21:5–7), we are to be reconciled to Christ. There is a powerful connection with the new creation through forgiveness. We see the effects of this reconstruction of our worldview into Christ Jesus in the Scriptures. Jesus points out this truth, even to those who are committed to remaining in the dead works of the past, and the strict interpretation of the Old Testament contractual covenant of the law.

"Which is easier, to say to the paralytic, 'Your sins are forgiven,' or say, 'Rise, pick up your mat and walk'? But that you may know that the Son of Man has authority to forgive sins on earth… He said to the paralytic, 'I say to you, rise, pick up your mat and go home.' He rose, picked up his mat at once, and went away in the sight of everyone" (Mark 2:9–12). Jesus is revealing to us in this text that to be forgiven is to stand as a healed person before His Father and everyone else. It's a witness to the new creation at work in us. We now stand before God and each other carrying our mat as a trophy of the new creation. What had been a sign of our weakness and frailty in the broken worldview of sin and death is now to be paraded around for all to see. We have been forgiven of our sins, and we are to forgive one another. Healing came to the paralytic in that moment when the past life of a sick man met the experience of the Word of Jesus both to heal and to forgive sin, and a new creation rose up and greeted a new future.

A person who lives in the worldview of reconciliation will not want to offend God or their neighbor because it isolates them and puts them back into fear and hurt. It locks them up into the small cell of limited understanding, pride, and emptiness, which is the worldview of sin and death. There's only one antidote to the confusion that's so easily swallowed by today's culture. It requires a regular self-examination of our conscience. If we feel fear, hurt, disappointment, and anxiety float into our soul attempting to sit down and replace our resting in the arms of Jesus, we should be self-aware enough to notice. It's appropriate to have a solid defense and make conscious choices in the Spirit to remain in the kingdom of the new creation (Gal.5:22–26).

So much of the New Testament is about re-framing our worldview. Our moral theology needs to embrace the reality of what Jesus is doing to invite us to a change of mind and heart and to cultivate our life in the new creation. Reconciliation is the key element of moral and ethical development and nurture, and throughout the Gospel, we see Jesus doing just that: "Do not judge and God will not judge you" (Matt. 7:1–2) and "The measure you dole out to others will be measured back to you" (Matt. 6:14). He tells us to "love our enemies" (Matt. 5:43) and to be kind and caring like the Good Samaritan, whom the Jews considered as outsiders; and to be great, you must be a "servant"(Jn. 13:12–15).

Jesus confronts the majority opinion about Jewish dos and don'ts with a prayer of reconciliation, the Our Father. It's meant to be a knockout blow to the dominance of any moral code that skirts around trust, forgiveness, and hope. God's solution for us is to live under His umbrella of reconciliation and forgiveness and to bless others with the same covering. A person aligned with Jesus in the new creation will be a witness to the power of forgiveness. They will experience it in their life and will extend its release and grace to others.

When the worldview of society's cultural gods, egos, and judgments comes into contact with the worldview of the new creation in Christ, there's going to be conflict. I had an experience that drove this truth home to me a number of years ago.

The bishop had asked me to be an interim pastor to a congregation that was transitioning from a rector who had retired after many years of service. They were going through a difficult change and were struggling. After I had been ministering to them for several weeks, it became clear that part of the problem was with some staff. I consulted with the bishop, and he supported the changes that I thought needed to be made. These decisions, although not uncommon, caused quite a ruckus. I let several staff people go, and it led to a meeting of the parish, the bishop, and me. A woman during the meeting, whom I considered a friend, got up and delivered a nine-page speech denouncing my decisions and my ability to pastor the church. I felt hurt and shocked by her words. A vote was taken, and it ended up that I would stay. The next week, that lady was not at church. She came back the following Sunday in a wheelchair. She waited for me after the service, and I went over to her and asked her what happened.

She said, "After the meeting two weeks ago, I went home and got ready for bed. I slipped off the bed by accident and landed right on my knees. I've not been able to walk since then. I want to tell you that I am sorry for what I said about you. It was full of half-truths, and I should have talked to you privately about my feelings. Will you forgive me?"

I replied, "Of course I forgive you as Jesus has forgiven me." I gave her absolution, and we prayed together, and then I said, "Stand up and walk!" She got up immediately without pain while praising God. She came back to church the following weeks totally healed.

Reconciliation is not about avoiding conflict, but rather, it carries us through conflict and change by God's grace. Before Jesus was born, there was conflict over Him. Jesus tells us that he will be a stumbling block for many, that He has come to bring a sword into the battle for humanity's soul (Matt. 10:34–39). It seems that wherever He goes, conflict shows up, even in His hometown and with His relatives and neighbors (Luke 4:28–30). Certainly we don't want to be the cause of conflict, yet we should not be surprised by it. The clash of worldviews produces this abrasive confrontation. When this happens, as it is now, and as it has before, we need to be encouraged and stand our moral ground. Reconciliation does not mean capitulation to the cause of this conflict, but it compels us to stand with Jesus and the new creation even when persecution comes (Matt. 5:11–12).

Reconciliation requires the consent of both parties to forgive, absolve, and change their behavior (repent) and heal the breach in their relationship. We were in no spiritual condition, because of Adam's sin, to give consent to our own redemption. Even if we could have, our will was so polluted by the effects of sin on our nature that we would not have done so. The apostles, for example, in spite of their best intentions, were absent at the cross. His own disciples abandoned Jesus. The Father needed a person to give consent in our place—a surrogate, someone willing to lay down His life and who freely was in a spiritual condition "without sin" to give consent for us.

I'm a hospital chaplain, and it happens sometimes that a patient is so sick, he or she is unable to give consent to a lifesaving procedure. Their surrogate speaks for the patient with their best interest in mind. They give the consent, or not, that the patient would decide if they were competent. Our redemption in Christ is like that. Sin has made us spiritually incompetent before God. Jesus made the decision of redemption for us. As both God and man, Jesus alone can fill the cup of our brokenness with God's salvation. We are reminded by Paul that "He made peace through His death on the cross" (Col. 1:20).

The effect of reconciliation is peace. When both sides have come to terms and have given consent, then peace is reestablished. The peace the Father gives as a benefit is to regain our lost standing as God's family, as His sons and daughters. Through the death and resurrection of Jesus, we are brought into the Father's new creation without our human initiative. That is why it's so vital for us to choose Jesus as our savior and follow Him. It's the only kind of consent we can give, and it's the way we enter into peace and reconciliation with God and one another. Through God's grace, which is now available to everyone, we affirm and accept what was done for us by Jesus's consent to suffer and die on the cross. We receive the benefits of the new creation won for us by the new Adam. The Holy Spirit leads and guides us as His community, now and forever, into the new creation of the Father's eternal blessings. We inherit the Father's worldview of making all things new and establishing unity through Christ by making us one in Him (Col. 1:15–23). We become like Jesus with the music of grace, the Father's dance of eternal life, the rhythm of holiness, and following Him as the Spirit leads. The outcome of our reconciliation to God through Christ Jesus in the Spirit is that God's grace makes us ambassadors of reconciliation to others. A person who is living in the Father's life and glory will be living in reconciliation. Being alive in the new creation requires the character of living in forgiving. There is no avoiding the forgiving character of the Father's blessing. Jesus is the worldview through which we receive adoption into everything so that Christ may be "all in all"(Col. 1:20). Jesus's forgiveness of sin and His victory over its effects, through His life, death, and resurrection, present us with daily choices to live as He does and to forgive as He forgives us. Living in the Spirit is to be liberated from the worldview of corruption and to live in the cradle of the new creation.

    An often-overlooked benefit of this new life is the re-acquisition of our innocence. It was lost because of the effects of sin, going back all the way to Adam and Eve in the garden. I have witnessed firsthand through inner healing, my own and others, the moment when a person experiences "the new Adam's love and forgiveness." It's like being born again (John 3:1–31). The old worn-out patterns fall off a person's soul. The alignment with past destructive alliances collapses, and the worn-out scripts of rehearsed hurts and griefs are healed. Suddenly, at that moment, a person is made new again. Reconciliation in Christ brings His new creation. It also restores our lost innocence. It makes freedom from sin not a someday hope, but a present reality. Every person is going to be tempted to slide into the corrupted worldview of self-absorption and fatalism. People aren't always loving or faithful, nor do we easily escape past pains, betrayals, hurts, and fears. The process of living in the new creation brings into focus the life of reconciliation. It opens us up to a new incredible adventure, a new life of freedom and caring (Rom. 8:31–39).

Caring for God's people, and His creation, is the important extension of the particles of God's moral framework won for us by Christ. I like to draw and paint. If I took ten artists, each looking at the same subject, with the same lighting, and even the same media, there would be ten different pictures. They would contain the same subject matter, but the character and expression of each artist's work would be different and unique. The reason for this difference is that we experience the world though our own individual lens of both subjective and objective reality. The fusion of these two perceptions along with the artist's skill with the media produces a synthesis that unconsciously connects with the person viewing it. Their recognition sounds like this: "I really like that painting." The art merges with our spirit, the fusion of the admirer's subjective and objective reality, and their unconscious. The work resonates with the cords of the new creation, and we say, "Isn't that beautiful." God sees us through the lens of His Son in every possible way. He knows us in all the facets and dimensions of our choices, our history, and our experience; and He loves us without conditions.

There is nothing so beautiful on this earth as a person caring for another person—a mother or father holding a newborn child, nurturing and bonding with that tiny person, or a volunteer at a nursing home listening intently and lovingly to an old person, even if they can't hear or see or remember their kindness. The Gospels show us how Jesus is drawn to people who need care. He always gives the time, energy, prayer, touch, forgiveness, and affirmation that are needed. We see, feel, and hear the beauty of the works of the Father in the ministry of Jesus. The works of God are the patterns of caring. Discipleship comes straight from Christ's heart of love. The new creation is awakened by the caring of God's people. We are drawn into a deeper experience of the Trinity the more we care for one another (Jn. 6:29).

I have worked in hospitals for many years. There is a big difference between a nurse, for example, who cares and is paid for their time and one who is paid without a sense of caring. It's also true for clergy, doctors, congressmen, plumbers, or presidents. When the motive becomes personal gain, work becomes a drag, a chore, something to escape. Patients and their families know when someone is caring or when someone is performing a duty to be paid. It's a subtle switch when our tiredness or burnout or personal pain or our culture's values make us somehow unavailable to care. It can happen without notice, just like it did to the Pharisees in the Scriptures. The greatest testimony about Jesus is that no matter how much pain he was in, he continued to care. He made no excuses, no angry avoidance, no self-protection. He heard the prayer of the repentant criminal being executed on the cross next to Him. Through the noise of the crowd, the jeers, the insults, and blasphemy, He listened to another broken heart. Even in suffering, the new creation bursts into its clearest view for us to see. Over hell itself, a voice of belief resonates down the long hallway of our history; it's remembered today and celebrated on Good Friday: "Today you will be with me in Paradise" (Luke 23:43). Jesus is the Son of God who cares, who forgives, and who dies to bring the new creation to life.

    I confess that there have been times when I have tried to escape the burden of being caring all the time. I have felt the weight of expectations press against my human limitations. It's so easy to become shallow and self-absorbed. We must resist the culture's case against trusting in God. The sentence of death is upon everyone. The broken promises that death's culture sells as a short-term antidote have never kept us from the grave. Caring in Christ is the only option that produces abundant life now and life everlasting. The more we care for others, the more the new creation in Christ grows inside our consciousness. We recognize Him in ways we never knew until we cared.

> I feel a stinging tiredness that time is almost over.
> It's a challenge to gulp down air, yet grasp the prize.
> Arms locked across my chest, clutching life's preserver
> kicking and straining, hard against the tide.

Chapter 10

Attitudes of the New Creation

Freedom for many, in today's culture and moral climate, is simply the natural state of humanity's self-interest apart from the demands of any higher divinity or good. It's not God, however, who has placed the performance anxiety of corporate advancement, for example, as the bar of success. Moral or ethical freedom is not an escape from God's demands and expectations. Real freedom is just the opposite. It's the ability to make good choices that are in union with God's purposes. Choices that are made based on the culture's values and expectations are easily politically and psychologically manipulated. The egocentric notion of many is that God is the problem and must be worked around or ignored. The secular worldview fancifully holds that if we could be liberated from God, then the culture and our human "will" would suffice as our moral compass. Once the connection with ontological goodness is vacated, there is no ground for our moral home (Matt. 7:24–27). We are left with only ourselves and the shifting sand of situational ethics and hedonism. Any kind of economic or political system built on these ideas, beginning with communism, fascism, and materialism, produces far less freedom than they promise. Even though they fail to make good on these expectations, human folly keeps digging them up trying to resurrect them. The other cultural option is to set up a ruling theocracy. It offers a simplistic answer that denies humanity and free will. It imposes a counter cultural cult like society for those who belong to the accepted sect or religion. It has been tried and is still failing. In the Middle East, for example, war and carnage have been going on for one thousand three hundred years. The Gospels tell us that Jesus taught, "His Kingdom is not of this World" (John 18:36). Christians can take great solace in this statement. Jesus is not about building a society to replace or reinvigorate the legalistic worldview with more controlling laws and elitist self-protection. The corruption of our politics, institutions, churches, and governments has no defense. We still sadly live with wars and rumors of wars, crime, exploitation, and the misuse of power, greed, and all the other forms of sin.

The worldview of Jesus is shaped by Isaiah 52–56, "The Suffering Servant." He lays down His life for us so that we may live. The credo of the new creation is to "love one another as I have loved you" (Jn. 15:12). It makes no social justice promises or societal evolutionary pledges. It leaves the choices of caring and loving one another centered in the orbit of Jesus's love for each person. We must take this calling personally. There is no equivalent program that can somehow claim the moral high ground or any human project that can repair the world. The church is built on the person of Jesus Christ, and in Him we find the meaning (grace) to make moral decisions. Does this mean that the church cannot speak to the culture and the dominating powers that seem to be running things? No. On the contrary, as God's people who live in Christ, we are empowered by the Spirit and celebrate the Father's love. We have much to say and to offer to a world that is broken and deluded. How should this categorical imperative, "Love one another as I love you" (Jn. 15:12) operate in making moral and ethical choices? How can it make a difference?

I believe that Christians can make a difference in the world for good. The life and the person of Jesus Christ, in the Spirit, will evoke out of the believers' heart a personal response called ministry. We see this in the formation Jesus gives His disciples. When they had known Him long enough, seen His miracles, heard His teaching, and been reconciled, He sent them out to minister His Word (Luke 10:1–12). The calling that Jesus gave them was for the sake of each person. He was going to suffer, die, be raised up, and redeem everyone. The dying and rising principle, as St. Ignatius calls it, "consolation and desolation"(Exercises of St. Ignatius) is the rhythm of the heartbeat of caring for every believer. Ministry is the experience of God's kinetic spiritual power to love and care for people in the Holy Spirit. Consolation and desolation, dying and rising, giving and receiving, forgiving and healing, (Tillich, 1975 edition) resonate with the polarities and pattern of Christ's own heartbeat. The church's task, our task, is not to attempt to recreate the world into our idea of God's order, but to cherish the new creation in Christ's heart and minister in it. The new creation is alive in every Christian who cares for others. An act of kindness, a generous gift, a listening ear to someone in pain, brings us into that new country of God's salvation in Christ. We find real meaning when we care for someone, because both parties experience the benefits, in the Spirit, of the new creation. The church speaks clearest as individuals and as a community to the world by genuinely caring for others. This "Theology of Caring in Christ" (Savage, 1996) explains the nature and content of God's love and revelation to the world. Love and caring translate the Father's communication, by prayer and action, through personal experience into the present moment and into reality.

What Is Caring, and How Do We Identify It?

When we look at the Gospels, we recognize several elements that are essential in providing real care to someone. First and foremost, caring reflects the qualities of Jesus. It's not a static set of external laws or rules, or even goals. Real caring is congruent with the believer's and the church's experience of Christ's love. Caring comes through grace, and it conforms to the qualities of Jesus's concern for every person. It's aligned with the caring, teaching, and life of the Master. Jesus's story—from the healing of the widow's son (Luke 7:11–17) to the Good Samaritan (Luke 10:25–37)—is His empathy and awareness for someone else in pain or distress. Jesus identified with both the sorrow of the widow and her loss, and to the Samaritan who first saw and helped the man who fell among thieves. The most important element in caring is to recognize that someone is hurting. Conversely, the most damaging hypocrisy is to pretend that the situation is not that bad, or to excuse ourselves from the unpleasant reality of pain, loss, hurt, fear, and sorrow, or to deny that there is anything wrong. It's obvious that we can be conscious or unconscious about the needs of someone else. Again, in Luke 16:19–31, we have the story of the rich man and poor Lazarus who suffered and didn't even get the scraps from the wealthy man's table. What is so important about this text is how the rich man never noticed the needs of someone he saw quite often. I have encountered my own inattentiveness to others around me. It usually occurs because of self-absorption. Instead of being aware of one another and noticing the other person, we bury our heads in the sands of i Pads, cell phones, and other electronic devices, or our own emotional or physical concerns. It seems that instead of opening up our world, we hold on to a smaller and smaller lifeline that limits our attention to only what we can hold in our hands.

Caring for one another in Christ gets us out of our comfort zone and into God's engagement with each one of us. Jesus talks about it by giving your coat to a person who just wants your shirt or walking an extra mile with a person who needs a friend. The way we can tell if we are caring in Christ is if it costs us something, our time, our treasure, and an investment of ourselves (Luke 6:27–31).

I have had to move often in my career. Moving is one of the most difficult things a person can go through. It's right up there with major losses, as far as stress goes. I have helped a lot of people move, especially when I had a truck. I find it quite amazing who shows up to help someone move. It's often not the people who said they would come over to help. It's often the unexpected help from a friend of a friend or someone in the neighborhood who was just passing by. When that surprise person or persons show up, they're often the ones who work the hardest.

I remember when my family and I were moving to a small-town parish in rural Texas, I was going to be the new vicar of the Episcopal church. We got there as evening was falling. We had packed up a big U-Haul truck and had driven all day through the worst rainstorm I have ever seen. It was the first time that I saw a dark green tornado sky. It was really ugly as if the world was going to end. Well, we made it and arrived mostly in one piece to the vicarage. We started off-loading the truck. A couple of people from the church showed up but didn't stay long. By that time, it was dark, and cars kept driving by with their lights on, and there was a steady stream of slow-moving traffic going by our house. I said to my wife, Dorothy, "This must be a very busy street. Look at all the cars driving by!"

She replied, "No, honey, they're not driving by because the street is busy. They just want to see who the new people are that are moving into town." Not one person pulled in and offered to help. I learned a lot about the church that day.

This little story shows that other motives can get wrapped up in caring. We can be curious or motivated by greed or ambition or religious superiority and seem to be caring. It creates a kind of ego reward that is really about ourselves and not about the person in need of help and care. Similarly, the person being cared for can manipulate the caregiver. The person being helped can use their weakness to guilt and extort from others what they can and should do for themselves. The Gospels show us the danger of this kind of fabrication. Caring in Christ will provoke an inner dialogue about our motives. It's not supposed to be a compulsive altruistic need to gain heaven. It comes out of the heart of Christ's love extending out to us. Real caring gets behind the mask of self-protection and selfishness. It opens up a conversation that is safe and gives physical, emotional, and spiritual support for the person to experience God's love.

We can tell if the ministry is really Christian caring or not by the fruit it produces. St. Paul mentions the fruits of the Spirit (Gal. 5:22–24), which are the trademarks of caring in Christ. These fruits propel us through grace to live in the new creation (Matt. 7:15–20). When the fruit is good, we enjoy its flavor, and we feed on its sweetness. It's the new wine of Cana that won't run out, and it's poured into our souls and gives us the taste of eternity. Compassion, kindness, gentleness, and beauty sing the song of redemption and praise in our hearts. If the fruit produced is bitter, self-centered, and demanding of others instead of serving their needs, it's empty and devoid of meaning. If caring is a ruse to ingratiate ourselves, or to manipulate others to gain power, or to puff up our ego, then it's not caring but a care-taking pretense.

How Do We Care for Someone?

Caring starts with small acts of kindness. There are opportunities available to us every day. We need to be on the lookout for them because they are so obvious. It can be that person who looks lost and needs directions or someone sitting alone in a cafeteria. It can be a stranger or someone whom we have known a long time. The Word of God teaches that we should be conscious and spiritually aware of what's going on around us. Jesus is in tune with the pastoral situation all the time. He stops to talk to the woman at the well (John 4:1–43) or notices Zacchaeus up in a tree (19:1–10). Time after time, He picks the fruit of redemption right in front of our eyes. Over and over again, Jesus brings caring into every personal interaction. The new creation bursts forth with each encounter changing, healing, forgiving, and caring. We experience the Word made flesh that now dwells among us. Jesus's ministry of caring begins with the person who is close by. Sometimes they came up to Him needing healing for themselves or a family member, or sometimes He was aware of someone who didn't realize that they needed His healing touch. Jesus seemed to find, or be found, by people in need of His Father's healing or deliverance. When He sends out the seventy-two, it's with the requirement that they follow his example. Christian caring begins with the people closest to us. It extends itself outward from there to the greater community (Luke 10:1–12).

My wife's body is interred in a beautiful mausoleum. I visit it about once a week. One day in my prayer time, it came to me that I could say mass there for her once a month. I received permission to have the service from the mausoleum staff. I thought, *Lord, I need to have some people there to celebrate communion. Who should I invite?* The thought came back, *Don't worry, I will invite them. You just celebrate mass.* I got there on Sunday afternoon after my usual morning service. I was alone. I set up the altar, which was already there because they often have funeral services and sat down. I didn't have to wait long. Just then a car pulled up, and an older Hispanic gentleman and his wife got out and walked toward me. I stood up and asked them if they would like to join me in offering mass for my wife. Then I asked them if there was someone they would like to remember. They told me that they had come to remember their son who died. He was a Down's syndrome child whom they took care of for over fifty years. They shared about his condition and how much they loved him.

Then they told me, "We have not gone to church for a number of years, and we need to go to confession."

I said, "Are you sorry for your sins?"

"Oh yes," they replied.

"Well, that's good enough for me, and the church. Please feel free to come to communion."

Since then, we have celebrated mass together several times. Now they are part of my family. They took care of Christ by taking care of their son. They had communion with God every day. I am so blessed to be able to offer them the Eucharist, as they remember him. Jesus has invited them to His banquet. Caring for Christ starts right with the people closest to us. This couple didn't know that they were ministering to Jesus, but He knew. They didn't know that He had forgiven their sins, but He knew. They didn't know that He would feed them at His table, but He did.

Living in the new creation is an active participation with God's plan in Christ to bring all things together in Him. Caring for one another is the means for growing into the worldview of God's redemption. It's to live dedicated to sharing, defending, and promoting the life of the Father's grace in the Spirit. It's an ever-growing attention to human life and creation as the expression of the love of God. The heart of Jesus shifts us from the worldview of law, culture, false science, scarcity, and deceit into the worldview of Jesus to live in the Spirit of love and caring. As St. Paul says, "We have been transferred from the kingdom of darkness into the kingdom of light" (Eph. 5:8–10).

The Attitude of Caring in Community

Most people have some idea of what kind of church they're looking for. It's often found deep inside our childhood experience. Our concepts of family are built from our history, either good or bad, and the church is often equated with our past familial relationships. A pastor may not know what a person is looking for when they attend church. Newcomers are rarely in touch with their expectations, but they still have them. Churches are vulnerable places because they unconsciously touch our need for belonging, safety, and understanding. These needs can be heightened by stress, losses, and life transitions. When life is painful, these times of powerlessness can prove overwhelming. When pressures come, we easily revert to the patterns that formed our personalities. What did we need from others, and what was withheld or given? When love was withheld in our family, it's easy to so desperately need it that the church becomes our personal territory of power: "This is my church, and nothing is going to change it." The other response is that since we didn't get the love and attention we needed in the past, "let's just give up having any expectations of caring." Any pastor, priest, or minister worth their salt has experienced this phenomenon. It takes some small, often unintended offense to cause them to leave the church. Past pain exists within all the families of parishioners; and sometimes these fears, losses, and hurts are lived out in the church.

I've been a priest for forty years, and there seems to be no clear-cut answer to the church's dysfunction. I do have a few things that I've learned. The New Testament shows Jesus calling a group of twelve to follow Him. There were no guarantees that they would stay faithful, and in fact, one of them turned Jesus over to the authorities who arrested Him, and everyone fled except John. What happened after Jesus died and rose from the dead? They kept meeting. I wonder why. Something was promised to them. Somehow the story was not over. Meeting together kept a thread of hope alive and gave them a chance to gather, to wait, to pray, and to support one another. There in the "upper room" when the light and glory fell on them, as they prayed, the community came alive too (Acts 2:1–4). It had always been about Jesus before, going where He led, listening to His sermons, experiencing His healing ministry. Now it was about them, because the Spirit had filled them with the possibilities of freedom, grace, and holiness. It was not the old wine of the law that bubbled into their hearts and minds. It was the new wine of the Holy Spirit that came with the glory and the fire of the new creation. The message Jesus preached was their message, His healing ministry was their ministry, and they would follow as the Holy Spirit led them like Jesus.

The Spirit came to each one of them, and it was this common experience that bound them together. So often the church is tied together by the personality of the priest or pastor. Too often the church is knotted together by laws and rules that attempt to do what only the Holy Spirit can do. Living in the new creation means living in community, not built by human hands, but fashioned by the Holy Spirit. This is not to say that the minister or pastor cannot have a good personality. On the contrary, a loving and caring pastor models the meaning of living in the new creation. This is not to say that the church cannot set boundaries for behavior or should give up its moral responsibility to live out the Gospel in an ethical and orderly way. It is to say that we cannot build or base community on these things. Community takes an internal, and spiritual, intention by each person to live in the Spirit, to love one another, and to live in the principles that St. Paul envisions as community life (1 Cor. 11:23–33) and that affirms our unity in Christ living in the Spirit. (Jn. 17:20–25).

The local church can grow so big that its ministry can be inhibited by the financial needs, of keeping the lights on, and of paying the staff, and growing the program, in a vain attempt to keep the congregation happy. Living in a pastoral care community requires a new creation worldview. It has a different focus from the large corporate or institutional paradigm.

Pastoral Care Chapels

The *pastoral care communities* that I believe will emerge and multiply are small groups. They will be like "chapels" of no more than eight or ten people that share a life of ministry. It may be to the sick or imprisoned, the poor, or the brokenhearted. They will gather, at least once a month, for prayer and mutual support. These chapels can be either interdenominational or of the same Christian faith. Belonging to a chapel will not mean that the participants would have to leave their larger churches. They may be very active in the ministries of a corporate-size congregation. The chapels will be for ongoing training and for prayer and support. Active listening (Savage, 1996) training is a basic requirement so that the members will know how to listen to each other. They might be part of a larger extended community called an Oratory. This will be the model for an organizational umbrella that provides quarterly ongoing educational events, coordinates activities, and serves as a connection to all the chapels that are working in the field of ministry.

Instead of a tree with lots of big branches but only a few leaves, let's spread out and have lots of leaves and not so many branches. Without the leaves, the tree withers and dies. Young people are dropping out of church in record numbers (Gallop, 2019). Perhaps a more intimate type of small group "chapels" model would be more responsive to this generation's need for bonding and belonging. Smaller groups that are trained to care for others are also an important response to cultural and societal pressures and discrimination.

> Amid this fugue, a tiny voice breaks through.
> The sound is hard to hear, yet so familiar.
> The faint and distant symphony of tender things I knew,
> a memory of bliss, a will of the wisp, a whisper.

Chapter 11

The New Adam

When God created man and woman, He set them in the garden with one commandment to obey: "Not to eat of the tree of the knowledge of good and evil" (Gen. 2:16). Adam and Eve's sin opened up the floodgates of laws and rules. Human beings needed to be kept in check and goaded into some kind of civilization or society. Moses gave the people of Israel the Decalogue, and from it evolved our common law. Jesus refers to Himself often in the Scriptures as the "Son of Man." The title that He uses marks out the territory of the new Adam. Unlike the first man, He obeys the Father's will perfectly. He removes all the laws imposed upon us a consequence of Adam's fall from grace. He gives us one new commandment, "To love one another as I have loved you" (John 15:12). Our choices for what we do, how we behave, or what we affirm and defend, or do or not do, must be in communion with Jesus.

It's tempting to try to use the new commandment as a standard with another set of rules and laws. For example, applying this principle to euthanasia, or capital punishment, might easily create an external rule that needs to be defended by an argument and enforced by external consequences. This would make the new commandment dependent on some authority to interpret its application to each situation. I want to consider instead the a-priori meaning of the categorical imperative of Jesus Christ. "Love one another as I love you" (Jn. 15:12) is a framework of God's grace that moves us into the new creation. Moral decisions and actions cannot be divorced from the person of Jesus. Our choices either align with Him or don't. Any discussion about euthanasia, or crime and punishment or race discrimination for example, with principles based on a set of personal or ideological foundations or premises, may rub up against the new commandment; but they will fail to be united to it because they lack the revelation of the new creation in God's Word and because human behavior is not simply an intellectual exercise. So much of the biblical narrative about Jesus along with Paul's writings, speak often about how to behave in a moral or ethical way but these teachings are just philosophical guidelines if they are not grounded in the person of Jesus (Jn. 15:1–18).

Jesus is speaking to us in the Spirit, through the Gospel authors, from His experience of the Father in the new creation. The first chapter of John's Gospel is focused on the pre-existent Word of God made flesh. The teaching of Jesus is not His own but comes from the Father. He is only doing what the Father is doing (John 5:19–23). His words and works are not His own but reflect back to us, in our humanity, the precious gift of the Father's love. When Jesus teaches, heals, and speaks, it's not from a distant or faint smudge of God's greatness. Rather, He is the Word made flesh that is with us (John 1:14). We may hear Him as a faint or distant voice, but it's often because we are trying to listen through the filter of the expectations of our culture's laws and rules and mores.

When Jesus teaches about moral behavior, we can easily think it's about what we should do, rather than what or who we are. We are meant to be a new creation in Christ. If a person needs a list of moral or ethical rules to follow, there's always the common law. St. Paul talks about this in his letters. He's quick to place this correction, that obeying the law will get a person no further than knowing the failure they have in keeping it (Rom. 7:4–6). It will not provide an entrance into the heart of Jesus and into the new creation. Living by grace, for St. Paul, is freedom "from the law," because the law cannot provide redemption from sin and its consequences. His teachings often include a set of moral contrasts over and against the requirements of Jewish law or religious rules and the moral code, *common law* and how Christians who believe in Christ should behave. He's not developing another set of legal requirements.

He is rather describing how the new creation is built on the morally freeing values of our Savior and our relationship with Him. Christians are often confused about moral choices because we try to keep a foot in both camps. We live in a world that runs under the constraints of many laws and rules. Yet the Gospel invites us into the new creation that has this major new categorical imperative. Paul is not describing a way out of keeping the law, but rather, a relational context of moral behavior in the Spirit that has risen over all laws and cultures in Jesus. Sin and death and the law cannot run the show anymore. The failure of the law to provide redemption is obvious. A relationship with Christ Jesus is the only possible alternative (Gal. 3:1–6). The new creation is open to those who believe not in the law but in Jesus through the Holy Spirit as the redeemer and the new Adam.

It seems so simple, at first blush, to recognize the necessity of our redemption in Christ and to avail ourselves of its benefits. Jesus, however, does not give a bottle of grace for us to satiate ourselves and to tightly withhold from others. Every choice we make that conforms to His grace opens us up in service to God and His people. Caring for others is always present when the new creation breaks in on us and as we live in it.

My family and I were living in a small town in West Texas when we somehow appropriated a couple of mixed-breed, medium-sized dogs. They were outside dogs and often found themselves on the front lawn of the rectory. Whenever a big truck or a car with bright hubcaps drove by, they would get all excited and chase them, getting real close, and barking and moving their heads around and around trying to bite the tires. They usually were quiet and got along well with others, but when a car or truck drove by, off they went like a shot. I wondered about their strange behavior, and one day the idea hit me. They probably misidentified those big shiny hubcaps as other dogs. They were confused by their own reflection. They were, in effect, chasing themselves. So often we are seduced by our desires and needs. We respond outwardly to our inner climate of personal needs, wants, and pleasures. Chasing our reflection round and around, trying to solve our problems and the world's riddles with our self-reflected view of law, ego, culture, and mythic science. We are unable on our own power to create for ourselves the freedom of the sons and daughters of God, no matter how we try to weave reality to serve our purposes (Peck, 2003 edition).

The new Adam speaks to us today from the new creation. The Spirit that raised Christ from the dead communicates the hidden mysteries of God from eternity into our time (Rom. 8). The New Testament Scriptures were written years after the Spirit had raised Jesus from the dead and after it had come upon the Church (Brown, 1968). Jesus tells us that He has to go so that the Spirit will come and lead us into all truth (Jn. 16:13). The virtues of faith, hope, and love and the charismatic gifts flow to us in the Spirit from the new creation. It's not a momentary look behind the curtain while the show is going on; rather, it's a full-blown invitation to enter into Christ's life in the new creation now and forever.

Moral choices are seldom purely private matters. Since we live in community with others, our choices affect others. The collision of personal interests, relationships, families, and social-religious institutions causes us to engage in common pursuits, political and economic interests, and professional concerns. All these and more are the expression of our common life. We make choices within the context of societal expectations and laws. We choose the values we live by. Jesus invites us to discover life's deeper meaning, not as a fearful, painful, and hopeless exercise but a joyful, loving, and meaningful relationship of grace. To appreciate the wonder of the gift of redemption and salvation, we need to see it from the Father's side, with His point of view. We know Him from the revelation of the Spirit in the new creation. The Scriptures are God's engagement, through the lens of our redemption in Christ, of the content of His love and care for us and all creation (Jn. 10:14–21).

Classical mystical theology defines the love of God and our love for Him as "holiness." The term "holiness" is compatible with the new creation. Another term is "union with God," which is also comparable to the new creation (Lagrange, 1948). Living in the presence of God's love and in His grace is not just a static ladder of spiritual advancement. It's not a destination of an impossible perfection that we only attain after we die. Living in the new creation is a dynamic experience of God's love in this moment. When we live in the new creation, through God's grace in the Spirit we are holy; we are in union with God.

The idea that God is so close to us sinners is hard to believe. It's not commonly taught. We know we can't somehow climb God's mountain of perfection and reach a mystical union with our Heavenly Father because of the problem of our sins. The culture's response to this is "If God is so unreachable, then why try at all?" Since we are all sinners anyway, and we can't deny our nature, then the quest for perfection is a pointless exercise. Many in the church believe that the best we can do is to try to be good enough for God somehow and rely on the mercy of Jesus to pull us out of the ocean of our sins at the end of our lives. The Scriptures tell us otherwise: trying to climb our own ladder to perfection is a waste of time. Jesus is the way. He is the ladder. Not only that, but because we are sinners, there is only one way to God. He is the gateway to live in the new creation. Jesus didn't come to place heavier religious burdens on our backs or to demand our human capitulation to God's transcendence.(Mt. 11:28–30). He came through his life, death, and resurrection to make us free from sin and death and raise us up as His sons and daughters. We are a new creation, and we are meant to make choices and act within this reality. When we act and trust in the Holy Spirit, we are living in the new creation, and we are holy because He is holy (John 11:25).

Today's culture and its values of power, fame, and self-importance and addiction drag human beings down into meaninglessness. They prop up false gods that are too distant and demanding, uninterested and nonexistent. It has only one central option to promote, which is that we buy what the world is selling. This attitude creates a spiritual entropy where God's voice, His revelation, is muted by the legion of other voices. These voices are far more entertaining, loud, mesmerizing, and attractive; but they don't provide a solution for our human condition. That's why the new Adam says, "That His sheep hear His voice, and will only follow Him" (John 10:16).

The entire moral climate that the culture produces is based on an illusion. It will never measure up to the fantasy it promotes by using cultural and mythic methods and symbols. Similarly, Christianity should not substitute one fantasy with another heavenly utopia. Many people claim to be Christians and believe in an afterlife, a place of heavenly rewards, yet this belief seemingly has very little effect on the choices they make. A belief in a faraway heaven is like a belief in a distant land that changes nothing in the land where I live. It often leads to a disconnect from the importance of the decisions I make today. If we are going to make real change, the choices we make are relevant in changing our inner landscape to reflect the beauty of that new country. It also means to take the risk to go and be there. Living in Christ means that with all the courage necessary, do not just dream or hope in that new land, but plan, engage, risk, and journey there. I must leave behind the things that can bog me down, face the uncertainty of an unknown future, and claim it for my own. I have discovered that believing in Jesus is to be a pastoral entrepreneur and to Join Him in ushering in that new creation.

I started Pastoral Care Associates (PCA) twenty years ago. I had no idea that it would blossom into a ministry that would touch so many people. I think we've ministered to hundreds of thousands of sick people, their families, and our medical staffs. Am I settled and retired in the knowledge that I have served, and now I need to rest? No, PCA is still moving into that new creation in new ministries. We seed that new land with the belief that more fruit will be produced, and each time we do, the new creation breaks in through the Spirit. We experience in the ministry of caring that new country of God's blessing, grace, healing, and eternal life.

Someone might ask, where do we confront the false worldview around us? The central problem of someone's resistance to living in Christ is the lack of commitment and participation in the Christian community. Being in a church is not meant to be a club or a fashion show or a place to somehow religiously mimic the culture's fascination with power, prestige, social acceptance and entertainment in a religious way. Living in the new creation will draw a person to participate with others in worship, caring ministry, community, and training because one of the ways we experience Him is in communion with others and by caring for one-another (Jn. 17:20–25).

It seems to many in the culture that when the church speaks about right and wrong or about moral or immoral actions, it places itself in a parental role and takes people back into the law that they cannot keep. We wonder how-to live-in grace and still have moral guidance and rules? Our culture looks at the history of the church and its moral teaching as hypocritical, since it has violated its own laws and rules. Many think of the church as irrelevant, just another taskmaster of judgment that enslaves people.

Recently I had a close friend die. He had asked me, as his health deteriorated because of cancer, if I would be the executor of his estate. I agreed, and this responsibility was noted in his will. There are quite a lot of rules and laws that need to be followed. The state is clear about those expectations. It was a real eye-opener for me. The more I got involved in all the necessary steps, the more anxious I became. How could I do this? Where will I get the time? How can I keep from making mistakes? I felt the weight and constraints of the law upon me. Then, I remembered my friend and how taking on this burden was a way of caring for him. If I stayed close to my friend's need and the grace of caring for him in this role, I will be blessed in the doing. This realization of service calmed my heart and brought me back in touch with the new creation.

When we live under the law and its burdens, it produces anxiety, fear, and worry to meet its requirements. The pressure to keep the law is always close at hand. If we, on the other hand, remember that we are living in the new creation, then we can recognize the real relational motives and the reasons for our choices. There is no escape from the expectations of the law that we must obey every day. However, living in the new creation frees us from being under burden of the law because of our bonding with Christ Jesus. The new creation is the experience of living in the freedom of the resurrection and in the power of the Holy Spirit as His sons and daughters (Rom. 13:1–13).

Principles for Living in the New Creation

Living in the new creation cannot be based on certain rules or laws that would put us back into the same old worldview that required our emancipation. We should not place legal requirements and limitations on the categorical imperative, which is to "love [care] for one another as Christ loves [cares] for us." (Jn. 17:20–25). A significant question we may ask is how do we make ethical and moral decisions that conform to the freedom of the sons and daughters of God in the new creation? Jesus didn't teach laws or rules, but He did teach principles that are important ingredients to living in the new creation. These elements are in harmony with the life of Jesus. Whereas laws and rules define the violation of the exercise of freedom and set consequences as deterrence, principles are relational attitudes. The person of the Holy Spirit reveals them and their application to the believer (Rom. 8:9–12). The virtues and the charisms that the grace of God produces in our hearts by the Holy Spirit provokes us to make decisions that are congruent with the person of Jesus. I am listing here some of the principles that come to mind. They are, by no means, a complete inventory of all the prime elements that Jesus taught. They are a significant set, however, that will bring to light the key spiritual qualities that lead us to our own appreciation of Christian moral teaching. Each principle beginning with the Beatitudes requires its own book. Many books have been written about these characteristics I am writing about an introduction to these qualities of Jesus from which we can see the foundations of moral and ethical decision-making. The first place we look is the Scriptures, and we find there in the Gospels of Matthew and Luke the principles of the Beatitudes.

Living in the Beatitudes

In Matthew 5:1–12, several things pop out when reading this teaching. Living in the Beatitudes means living in the character of Jesus. He is all those things—meek, a peacemaker, a person of righteousness, poor in Spirit, pure in heart, and persecuted for the sake of the kingdom (new creation). Each Beatitude starts with "Blessed are." This is not a legal prescription for action or inaction. It does not even require compliance. It rather identifies qualities that conform to the person who gives and embodies them. (Metz, 1968). The blessing comes in the living out of these virtues that are the characteristics of the new Adam who brings the new creation. A more complete explanation of its meaning is "Blessed are you when you are living in the new creation by being meek, or bringing peace, or being poor in spirit, pure of heart, righteous, and especially in facing persecution." Having faith in Jesus means believing in the new creation even when it seems hidden from our view. We become a living, walking, talking sacrament of the new Adam and the new creation in the Spirit.

Nowhere in the Gospels is there a demand placed upon us to go out and do the beatitudes. Rather, Jesus teaches us to "be" something; and by being in Him, we are harmonized and bonded in Christ to the new creation. This teaching is diametrically different from the requirements of the application of the law and the legal structures that codify and punish or reward human behavior.

Living in Unity

The next important principle is unity in Christ. In the book of Revelation, we are told that the opposites come together on that day of Christ's return. Revelation 21:ff. notes that there will be a new heaven and a new earth. There will be a marriage of Christ and His bride. There will be no death, tears, or grief or crying. God's home was on the throne, but it's now with mankind. Old things have disappeared; all is new. He is the beginning and the end. These opposites come together in Christ (Tillich, 1975). The merging of the opposites of our fallen humanity and God's holy perfection is reconciled by the new Adam who dies so that we may live. Jesus tells us in the Gospel of John that we should be one like He and the Father are one, like a vine and the branches are one, like friends who know each other and make plans together are one (John 15, 16, and 17).

Human beings keep trying to put the opposites in the universe back together again without God. We see after the sin of Adam, beginning in Genesis 11:1–9 with the Tower of Babel, that we have always fallen short. It's not possible, with human ingenuity and science, to create for ourselves the new creation. Sin and the effects of sin, particularly pride, gets in the way and limits the prospects of any utopian dream. Society, without Christ, falls back into the shallow facade of empty promises that the old law of sin and death cannot redeem. There are many scientific advancements, but they often open other unintended doors that lead to destruction. The benefits of atomic research, for example, and its benefits like electricity at the same time are used to create atomic bombs that can wipe out the world. Human hubris is like a vacant and forgotten lot of an old movie studio. It looks like buildings from the Old West or the 1920s on the outside, but if you walk around behind them, they are just empty scaffolds. They're just facades, not the real thing at all.

The only way to bring the "polarities" (benefits vs. liabilities) of our world together is to be one in Christ Jesus and to live in the Holy Spirit and in the grace of the new creation. It's true that science can cause us to postpone dealing with our mortality, but that day will come when we have to face the truth of life's temporal limitations. There is no cultural or scientific substitute for the new creation that Christ brings. Jesus tells us in John 3:16, "He has come to bring life." If we live in Jesus, then the Spirit will drive us into God's unity as surely as the Spirit led Jesus into His ministry (Mk. 1:9–12).

If we live in the new creation, we can expect resistance. The culture will fight back to hold its ground of failure and meaninglessness. The devil doesn't give up territory without a conflict. Paul's exploits in Acts point to the difficulty of knocking down the "strong man" that is promoted by the attractiveness of the culture's secular worldview (Acts 17:16–32). The "cultural elite" will make peace with any religion that can mute the Christian voice. They will go so far as to promote a religion that even ascribes hostile views of its own modern values so it can deaden the connection between Christ and His bride. They promise to make the world one through "globalism" without Christ. They promise to lift society out of its religious goo and produce unity without faith in Jesus Christ. They say, "What is needed is faith in ourselves." The myth of unity without Christ leads to violence. It trades the gold of truth for its fools gold of mere appearance. It requires the enforcement of nonsensical laws and metes out punishments that push us back into the devil's minefield of delusion and fear. The cultural elitist worldview is that "unity" cannot be "freely" realized, so it must be demanded and enforced. It must be manufactured and settled on the battlefield, in the courts, in the classroom, and on the streets.

Christ's priestly prayer flies in the face of society's nominalist polemic. Jesus knits together our life with His in being one with the Father. The Gospel of John,

17:21–22 reveals, "I pray that they may all be one. Father! May they be in us, just as you are in me and I am in you. May they be one, so that the world will believe that you sent me." It's a prayer for action and belief, not for someday or when the time is right. The prayer for unity is forged in the love of Jesus and fashioned in the Spirit right now in the new creation.

Living in Authenticity

The Gospels tell us that one thing Jesus confronted, over and over again, was the sin of hypocrisy. He had no stomach for it. The prophetic tradition in the Old Testament is also critical of the pretense of religious ritual at the expense of living a life of mercy and justice. Jesus is the real Messiah. He is the real Son of God and Son of Man. Living in the new creation means to be authentic. A believer is not to make a show of their good works, or to seek the place of honor, or to have power over others to manipulate them by intimidation (Lk. 6:17–26). Being an authentic Christian moves us in the Spirit to be transformed into a son or daughter of God. It is not a casual nod to the past, but a celebration of Christs presence in how we live now.

Sin moves us in the opposite direction, away from admiring God into admiring ourselves. It even blames God for our failures of measuring up to the Father's lawful and loving expectations. Sin causes us to give up hope in transcendence and replace it with the forbidden fruit of human frailty and our overripe fascination with meeting our own needs and justifying it with our intellectual rationalizations (Eph. 2:1–10).

There is nothing so beautiful on this earth as the admiration of a wife for her husband and a husband for his wife. It's a singular mystery that affirms and recognizes the sacredness of the bond between them. Often Dorothy would look at me in such a way as to convey without saying a word that she held me in such high esteem. It's not only physical love but a deep connection to our bond of unity, of value, and of dignity. Words fall short in describing this profound meaning. It's like gathering up in one basket all the experiences we shared together, the battles we have won, the victories and defeats, and the life we know to be ours, because we chose it and have lived it. Looking into her eyes and seeing that smile on her face translates an admiration that validates me. It said without words that she would do it all again because she held me in such high regard. The affirmation of love leads us to be authentic. The new creation bursts forth in the Father's admiration of His Son Jesus. Through His eyes in the Spirit, Jesus sees you and me in the same way, and the Father recognizes His Son in us. I must confess that of all the things I miss most about Dorothy, I miss that look of her admiration. So, I'm determined to live remembering that look every day and to celebrate it as my special gift.

The desire to be authentic is not a guilty self-depreciation of my worth. It's not another rule or promise I have to keep. Being authentic is a response to being so loved by God that I desire to be like Him. It's not a set of expectations whose goal is to measure up to God's perfection, but rather to live in the Spirit and in the new creation of our Father's admiration in Jesus Christ, (Lk. 3:13–17) which is perfect, holy, and new!

Living in the Spirit of Reciprocity

Jesus responded to the apostles' request to show them how to pray and gave them the Our Father. There is a reflexive edge to almost everything Jesus taught. He wants us to know that if you want to be forgiven by God, you must forgive each other. If you judge others, God will judge you by your same yardstick. The measure you use for others will be measured back to you. Living in the new creation is an acknowledgment that God's justice and love also bring accountability for the choices that we make (Luke 6:37–39). Clearly Jesus brings this teaching home to us when He says, "Do not judge others and God will not judge you; do not condemn others, and God will not condemn you (Matt. 7:1–3); forgive others, and God will forgive you (Matt. 6:14–15). Give to others and God will give to you. Indeed, you will receive a full measure, a generous helping, poured into your hands—all that you can hold. The measure you use for others is the one that God will use to you" (Lk. 6:37–40).

Life comes within a context of decisions. The consequences of action or inaction produce a fruit that can either be eaten and enjoyed or fill our mouths with a foul distaste because of its bitterness (Lk. 6:43–45). Living in the new creation is to be aware of this principle of reciprocity and to live in its freedom. If we reap what we sow, (Gal. 6:7) then it becomes important to plant the seeds of the new creation by loving and caring for one another.

We are to value the Father's justice by keeping it in sight. Justice is not a creation of the demands of culture, which seeks to create sameness as a way of removing responsibility for the chaotic nature of change. Real justice seeks God's equilibrium because change is not the enemy; rather, it's a revelation that celebrates the proclamation of the truth, and that truth is found in the person of Jesus (John 14:6). All the Gospel principles reveal the incarnation They are embodied in the person of Jesus who was and is both God and man at the same time. He holds perfect justice and mercy in His heart; and the calling for us, in the Spirit, is to do the same.

Living in Generosity

Generosity and thankfulness are equally yoked and married to the character of Jesus. He teaches, throughout the New Testament, these two spiritual principles in the same breath. We are blessed when we live in the recognition of God's generosity of providing the world for us as a gift (Lk. 11:9–12) The Spirit's purpose in giving us the new creation is that we acknowledge its benevolent intent and its quality from the Father's storehouse of His goodness. Jesus stands up for this worldview over and over again. Parable after parable pushes us into realizing the generous nature of God's grace. A person who appreciates God's goodness, in the natural world, will likely be thankful to Him for its creation.

Modern liberal cynicism is a result of not accepting God's generosity in creation. It grasps onto a sense of personal entitlement because it doesn't accept God's beneficent gift of the universe and our place in it. This mythic worldview keeps a record of wrongs against the environment and maintains fearful control over its assets as a way of managing humanity's footprint in the world. It tries to shape a world based on the notion that since the world's resources are so limited, only a few enlightened elite can decide for everyone else how to manage the cruel limitations that nature has handed us.

Jesus's teachings point us to the Father's goodness and generosity. If we accept God's benevolent nature, then we can begin to see his beneficence all around us. Without this belief in God's generosity, the world is a dangerous and vile place. The law of the jungle is the inheritance of a stingy or disengaged god. Jesus, by His life and teachings, death, and resurrection (the pattern of redemption), shows us his Father's munificence. If we accept the truth of the testimony of the early church, and we accept Jesus into our hearts through the Holy Spirit, we will be moved to respond lovingly to one another. Failure to be kind, loving, forgiving, faithful, and good stewards of creation by mirroring God's generosity is to be deprived of receiving God's benefits in the new creation. A faithful disciple is a person who believes in the heartland of the Father's kindness and acts that way. The experience of difficulties or scarcity or suffering can pose new opportunities to be generous, creative, and altruistic. Looking behind the curtain of our human condition, and its weaknesses, Jesus points us directly to God's generosity. We are to be like Him by thanking the Father for the beauty, complexity, and wonder of the world (Lk. 16:19–31).

The measure that is most important to us is time. If we are generous with our time, then sharing it becomes the architecture of friendship. A real relationship takes time to nurture and sustain. The gift of time to be with someone in pain or to listen to someone who needs attention takes us outside our own concerns. Taking time requires a generosity of spirit. Unfortunately, we can so fill up our time that we have none left to share with anyone. We can be so enamored by our mechanical devices, phones, and computers that we miss the time to reflect on life. If we crowd our minds with no time to spare and little time to give, we may miss out on the wonderful calling in our life of the new creation.

Living in Creativity

I love to paint and draw. Writing is a new adventure for me, one that brings its own frustrations. I wish, quite often, that I could type with my fingers what my brain wants to say. I have discovered even in this difficulty a discipline that causes me to patiently stop, write, and edit my work. Our talents are often the first place we discover our interaction with God's mystery. How did I paint that? Or how did I fashion that beautiful thought and write it down? Where did it come from? The artist, the poet, the musician, is affected by the surprise of his or her own work. Any creative endeavor that connects us to beauty and goodness is an inspiration of meaning that transcends our human condition. It ties us through grace to the new creation.

When I was a youngster, I would try to copy the drawings of the human figure by Michelangelo. They were poor attempts, but I continued to practice. My parents noticed my efforts and started calling me Michelangelo, like a nickname. Then it got shortened to "Michelang." It never bothered me; as a matter of fact, I enjoyed it. One day my dad and I were visiting a priest friend after Mass at the Cursillo Center. His name was Fr. Ambrosi, and he asked me if I would do a drawing, like a poster that he could use for his next retreat. It needed to be a picture of Christ and His suffering for our sins. I said okay and went home to work on this project. I started that night on a drawing, and what seemed to emerge from the paper touched my heart. It was a picture of Jesus with His arms outstretched looking directly at me, but He was behind a wall trying to get through it. The drawing was in perfect anatomical proportion. I drew the picture effortlessly, and it became clear to me that I was being inspired. The picture was beyond my humble ability to create. Yet there it was. It spoke to me of my resistance that kept His love from breaking through to my heart. I recognized that I was a sinner, and I needed to invite Him into my life and break down the wall that I had built. The tears began to come as this experience dawned within my consciousness. Jesus had communicated with me in a picture (visual experience) that had opened my heart up to feeling His love and tenderness (kinesthetic experience). Since that time, I have seen, heard, and felt His love and care too many times to count (Savage, 1996).

Art, music, writing, acting, dancing, and athletics are means that are deeply aligned with the heart of God's love for creation and our place in it. It opens us up to the mystery of life and its profound wonder. Real art presents us with God's grace to see, feel, and hear the things that come right from the new creation because Jesus makes all things new. The artist, poet, athlete, sculptor, and musician reveal through their experiences the unique content of God's plan of telling the story of the universe. (Psalm. 24 & 47)

Unfortunately, art or music, or any creative activity, can be idolized as an end in itself. It can be polluted as a means for fame or money, power or pleasure. God's love, on the other hand, enhances our ability to appreciate beauty and celebrate it in the arts. Whenever God's grace is at work, new and creative ways of expression emerge. Jesus used images like "the birds of the air, or the lilies of the field, or a pearl of great price, and bread and wine" to transmit the nature of His Father's love and faithfulness. When the artist, musician, or dancer paints, plays, or performs, the design of the Father's intention in creation itself can shine through. Jesus said it this way, when He was confronted by those who resisted Him as His parade entered Jerusalem (Luke 19:40) and they told Him to keep his followers quiet, "I tell you that if they keep quiet, the very stones themselves will start shouting." Creation is in harmony with its creator when Jesus is present. It shouts and praises God. It glorifies the designer of its complexities and simplicity. The Psalms are full of the witness of creation to the wonder of God's glory. He holds everything together in a kind of tension, like strings on an instrument that resonate with eternal splendor (Job 38 & 39).

> "Step into my Father's moonlit valley," it says.
> "Walk down the path and smell the perfumed air.
> Come closer, in the hollow of creosote and sage,
> the tingling garden of creation. Wait for me there."

CHAPTER 12

Free to Choose the Lord and the New Creation

Contemporary arguments about the existence and nature of good and evil often end up with an indictment of God. Either God is a Zoroastrian combination of both good and evil and therefore not to be trusted, or he exhibits a pagan callous disregard for creation. The result of this "straw god" attitude toward the divinity's motives, and actions, presents a false dichotomy. It's as if acknowledging the existence of evil is a symptom of God's foreknowledge and responsibility. It's like saying that the doctor who does surgery to heal a patient is directly responsible for everything else that happens to the patient from then on. If the patient does not follow the doctor's orders or is non-compliant with the treatment or medications, the responsibility for the outcome falls on the patient, not on the doctor. Our human tendency is to place blame, or judgment, on God for life's pain and difficulties, rather than accepting responsibility (Col. 2:6–11) for the consequences of our choices and acknowledging the reality of our human frailty.

The most important element of God's grace is the freedom to choose Him. Free will. The reality of our fragile human condition, namely, pain, suffering, and death, impacts the choices we make both as a society and as individuals. To understand sin, death, and evil, we have to start with the spiritual exercise of making good or godly choices. We often start in the wrong place. Instead of focusing our attention on the symptoms of society's ills, let's examine the nature of our choices where decisions are birthed and from which society is either nurtured or harmed.

The freedom to decide for ourselves is a power. It's often coveted by government, culture, and even religion. God does not covet our power to choose; rather, throughout the Gospels, Jesus affirms individual conscience. He goes to great lengths to foster and teach about the exercise of freedom. Most of the parables deal with choosing to do the right thing when there is societal-religious resistance. Good does not exist in a vacuum.

It's not just an intellectual exercise devoid of the context of life or human bonding. Jesus places the emphasis for choices on the nature of the relationship He has with the Father. He will not back down from affirming His bond with His Father. When He teaches about the Eucharist in John, we are told that many disciples thought His teaching was too hard or difficult to follow, and they left Him (John 6:25–59). Jesus leaves the door open for even the apostles to leave over His teaching. Jesus is inviting them to choose. He does not try to sell them or produce another miracle to convince them to stay. Jesus requires a free choice to follow Him. He recognizes that only a free choice, without coercion or fear, extortion, or intimidation, is required for commitment and that no real commitment is possible without free choice. The problem is obvious, if God is so gracious to guard our freedom, even to choose against Him, what causes human beings to do all in their power to limit and control the choices of others? Modern culture, government, and social and religious institutions seem to be the main culprits in shorting out our free will. Throughout history, we can recognize the prevailing winds of social, political, and cultural conformity. It's a staggering indictment when the state tries to steal from the individual their rights to the exercise of freedom. I'm not speaking here of removing laws or moral and ethical boundaries. I am suggesting that we can't rely on these external supports to provide the assurance that we are making free choices. Freedom resides in the truth, and that resides in Christ. Adults cannot depend on the externals of government or schools or social institutions or the media to protect them from the exercise of free will by making choices for them. Society can be so easily led astray or manipulated by these powerful forces.

Moral values are affirmed by living in Jesus, in His principles, and in the Holy Spirit that reveals the new creation. We will not be disappointed when our choices are allied with Jesus's principles, and we apply them to the moral issues of our day.

It's clear, from the Gospels, that living in the new creation sometimes means that believers may suffer, and they may not be appreciated or understood. Jesus tells us about picking up the cross and carrying it (Matt. 16:24). He points us to the Father by walking in our human sandals. Jesus tell us "that when we see Him, we see the Father" (John 14:9). The work of God's salvation involves everyone who chooses Him. It's not a choice that satisfies the shortsighted goals of power, success, or wealth. It's a choice that's a witness to a new and dynamic relationship that mirrors His relationship with the Father. Through the Lord's life, death, and resurrection and by living in the Holy Spirit, the same can be said about us, "when the world sees us it sees the Father" (John 14:9).

Many people have told me how much I look like my dad. It's true. I have some of my mother's facial characteristics too, but my fathers are the most dominant. When I was young, I wasn't aware of that fact. I was even in a little denial about it. Now that I'm older, and so is he, a stronger resemblance has emerged. I have the same plump belly and similar French nose and chin. There is more than just a biological affinity too; with age comes the experience of growing through life together. He shepherded me through my childhood and teenage years and into young adulthood. He has fashioned my history with his own. The patterns of his belief in God, his values, and his choices have etched their mark in the lines on his face and mine too. They contain the smiles and laughter, joy and celebrations, along with the hard experiences of change, and the weathered times of pain, sickness, and loss. I have come to the place where I not only know that I am my father's son, but can see it. If this is so in the natural order, think about how it's even more apparent with Jesus who perfectly reveals His Father to us in the Spirit.

Each choice that we make to follow Jesus leads us to be more like Him. We choose Him in the Spirit with His grace. We affirm the evidence of that choice in our Spirit and in our bodies. The freedom of these choices is essential to secure the bond of sacred trust in God's Word. Living in the new creation is to live in freedom.

If freedom is the single most important ingredient for the exercise of our will, then God's purposes are served by its maintenance. Paul in Romans 8:14–17 says, "For the Spirit that God has given you does not make you slaves and cause you to be afraid; instead, the Spirit makes you God's children and by the Spirit's power we cry out to God, 'Father! My Father!' God's Spirit joins himself to our spirits to declare that we are God's children."

The choices that we make should mirror His principles and are not solitary acts based on our own good intentions or self-satisfied requirements of the law. They flow from our relationship with Christ by His grace and from the Holy Spirit. It's the plan of God the Father to reveal His intention and love in creation through His Son in the Spirit (Eph. 1:1–23). It's the height of hubris for human beings to miss the evidence of God's glory while focusing on the insignificance of our own needs and desires. We are bent toward prevarication as a means to control God and to supplant His voice with our own. So many people are not sure if they believe in God. They don't see the connection between a belief in God as normative for our self-definition and the fruit of goodness and virtue. The Father's principles and intentions ingrained in creation are distorted and dismissed by their muddled and broken worldview. A person trapped in this moral ambivalence is not free. Many people avoid asking themselves questions that dig deeper into their own spiritual ground. They somehow believe that if I don't consider the question of God, I don't have to struggle with finding or needing Him. Considering the subject only causes more ambivalence. It's better not to consider it at all. The denial of God's relevance dodges our ability to make choices, because it dismisses our freedom and weakens our will to align with the Father's worldview and principles. I see this resistance so often in the hospital. Even the medical staff can view the chaplain as an unnecessary intrusion into their life-saving territory. When the chaplain comes to visit, families and patients say things like "I'm not going to die, am I?" or "Who sent you to see me?" or "I don't need a chaplain." All this resistance attempts to skirt around the issue of our mortality and our fragile nature. We don't want to feel our weakness, and the idea of God reminds us of eternal things. The world is passing away, and sickness makes the reality of our human condition all too real.

Jesus in the Gospels not only affirms free choice but also exposes the nature and significance of our choices. Jesus does not cover up, or minimize, the exercise of our free will. He affirms it and sanctifies it. He wants his followers to know what they are giving up and what they will gain: the hardships and the benefits of being a disciple. There are no excuses that allow us to put the choice of following on hold. "Let the dead bury the dead" (Matt. 8:22). No special deals that help avoid the consequences of believing and following. Because so much is riding on each choice, there can be no excuses or hiding from the importance of staying the course, being on the journey, being faithful to its promise, and growing in its grace. Jesus secures the choice to follow and to be sustained in it, as a "spiritual power." It requires a relationship with Him. The power of the new creation is the power of the Holy Spirit (Jn. 15:26–27). Jesus raises the nature of consent to follow Him and defines its costs and benefits, namely, the cross and the resurrection; but the power to live in it comes from the same Spirit that raised Him from the dead (Rom. 8:11). Once we have chosen to follow Him, then we need the Spirit to lead and guide us into the new creation. God does not challenge us. God invites us to choose. The challenge comes from our own desires to avoid choice and, morally or ethically, to quietly sneak out of town before the sun of decision goes down (Lk. 24:13–33). We attempt, like Adam and Eve, to hide in the bushes and blame each other for the consequences that come with choosing to live outside the new creation (Gen. 3:8–13).

The gravest assault on free will is slavery. It removes freedom as a choice and destroys the possibilities of an emancipated future. Slavery can take many forms: drug addiction, compulsions, overwork, violence, egoism, racism, and all kinds of sin. Jesus came into a world of slavery, people conquered in war, criminals of the state, or those who had lost their freedom being sold or bartered to remove a debt. Many of His parables use the slave as a central character. A slave is not free to come and go; to hold any kind of material, economic, or social power; or to even think for themselves, unless it's given to them. It makes a person a property. Slavery subjugates a person to the will of the owner or the state or the pimp or the drug lord.

Jesus doesn't demand a violent overthrow of the evil injustice of the state or those who barter with the lives of people. He seems, at first glance, to accommodate the system of His day, since He doesn't demand a violent overthrow of Rome. Even his own people in their history had been enslaved in Egypt and Babylon and by the Greeks and finally by the Romans. His plan is not to impose the kingdom of God by force. The contest of good and evil is decided by the choices made in the will of a person. Jesus models this inner battle beginning with the temptations in the desert after His baptism. To paraphrase what Jesus says, He is only interested in doing the will of His Father (Matt. 4:1ff). Doing the will of someone else can seem like a kind of slavery. However, slavery is a taking of someone's rights. Jesus gives to the Father His will to obey Him as a source of real freedom. It's not slavery to "freely" give to another person power over you because you love them. It promotes a submission and dependency to the other called "faith and trust." A society of the new creation would never be compatible with a social system that accepts or promotes any kind of slavery, because it denies the person's free will and the dignity and the purpose of God's creation and redemption (Jn. 8:34).

Jesus never seems affected by His relationships to treat the will of others in the same way as doing the will of the Father. We never hear Him say to the apostles, for example, "What do you think I should do?" or "Where should we go next?" or "How can we convince the people that I'm the Messiah?" Doing the will of His Father is the greatest freedom of all. It allows Jesus to bear up under rejection, misunderstanding, hatred, and finally suffering and death. Likewise, for the disciple, it requires the same decision to follow Jesus in the same way He follows and obeys the will of the Father (Jn. 14:6–4).

I entered the seminary after my first year of college. I had been very involved with the new "charismatic movement" that had begun to sweep the Catholic church in the early 1970s. The seminary was in California, and the renewal was just getting started there. I had led prayer meetings, and I was very excited about sharing this experience of the Holy Spirit with my fellow students. I went to the spiritual director of the college and asked if it would be all right for us to have a prayer meeting once a week in the evening. He was a slight and pale-looking priest who didn't seem all that interested, but he asked me a question: "What is a prayer meeting?" At first, I was a little taken aback, thinking, *What do I say?* So, I replied, "It's where we pray together, and we ask the Holy Spirit to give us a new language of praise and worship to Jesus. It's called praying in tongues. We sing and read the Scripture, and we share experiences of God's grace and the ministry of the Holy Spirit that happened to us during the week."

He said, "Well, I've never heard of such a thing. However, if you are willing to have one of these so-called prayer meetings, I think it would be important if the faculty was invited."

I answered, "It would be fine with me if they would like to come." We agreed on a day and time, and I got busy informing some students that we would be allowed to have our first prayer meeting. I was nervous but I was also looking forward to having our prayer group. The day came, and we met in one of the classrooms. I was very surprised to see that all of the faculty, except the rector, were there. We had several students too. I began by telling everyone, "We call this a prayer meeting, because that's what everyone who comes should be doing. It's not a place to be watchers, but to participate. If you are here to gawk or be entertained, you should really not attend." With that, I opened the meeting with a extemporaneous prayer and a Scripture from Paul's first letter to the Corinthians, chapter 12, and a short explanation of the gifts of the Holy Spirit. Before I could complete my little teaching, one of the students suddenly stood up and said, "I want to receive the gift of the Holy Spirit. Would you pray for me?"

I said, "Of course, please come over here and sit in this chair." He quickly got up and came over to the chair and sat down. I looked at him, and tears were already running down his face. "Okay," I explained, "we're going to put our hands on our brother's shoulders, and those of you who want to can come over and join me." I closed my eyes and started praying for him to receive the baptism of the Holy Spirit and for God to give him a new prayer language to praise Him. I started praying in the Spirit, and right away so did he. I looked down, and he had his hands up and was praying in the Spirit right along with me. His face was bright red, which went along well with his red hair. Tears of joy were streaming down his face. I looked around the room and saw that all the faculty had left. I thought to myself, *Well, I guess we scared the hell right out of them, Lord.*

The next week I heard back from the spiritual director. He told me that the faculty had consulted the cardinal and that there would not be any of this "praying in tongues" allowed if we were going to have prayer meetings. I had to give a weekly outline of the Scriptures that would be used, and an order of service placed under his door every week. I did this spiritual exercise for three years. Every new term, more and more students entered the seminary who had been baptized in the Spirit. Finally, a new spiritual director was appointed. He called me into his office one day and said, "Mike, we can't ignore your obedience. You have done everything you were told to do. You can continue to have your prayer meetings, and you can use all the gifts of the Spirit."

The baptism of the Holy Spirit is an immersion into the new creation. It's based on a personal conversion to Jesus Christ as Lord and Savior. It opens up the person's heart to experience an entirely new worldview. A person receives a new prayer language that comes from inside their spirit as the Holy Spirit anoints and leads them in prayer, praise, and worship. It's a major step into that lost garden of delights, recovered by the new Adam for us. It's a mystical experience that presents to the person the reality of God's love and His power to gift the church with teaching, preaching, prophetical word, healing, spiritual insight, discernment, and Christ's victory over evil. The Holy Spirit conveys these gifts for the building up of the body of Christ. The Holy Spirit also reveals them so that we might experience the homecoming of the new creation that sin subtracted from Adam and Eve. The baptism of the Holy Spirit along with the Word, prayer, and the sacraments are the milieu of living in the new creation right now (2 Cor. 5:16–21).

This little story also reveals how God's providence works. Change can happen in the world when we align our will with God's purposes, not the other way around. Good actions are begun with good decisions that come from a spiritual bond with Jesus in the Spirit. Good intentions are not enough to produce good outcomes. So often the desired outcomes get tainted with the human bent toward sin's self-serving protection. If we stand under the banner of Christ's victory over sin and death, we are in a different framework, a different worldview, a new creation. Good will and good outcomes are only possible by choosing to be dwelling with Christ in the Holy Spirit. If we choose to live in the Holy Trinity's relationship of freedom, then we are free. The freedom we have is not a license to break the law but rather a condition of surpassing its failure. Grace breaks the hold that the law has to constrain us to society's judgments and human limitations. The new creation is not a construction of human beings. It's the activation of "living in the Holy Spirit" that transfers us in Jesus Christ from darkness into light (Col. 1:13).

> Carefully, I went unsure, unsteady with each stride.
> I glanced side to side and focused my eyes all around.
> The cool evening fog secured me with its misty tie,
> not afraid of what I'd find, only hoping that I'd be found.

Chapter 13

Living in the Holy Spirit

If the Gospel takes us into the country of God's new creation, how do we speak to this fractured world? We know from the Scriptures that the world is passing away. The "new creation" will take its place: "Sin and death will be no more, neither will there be grief, crying or pain. The old things have disappeared" (Rev. 21:4). Like a child developing in its mother's womb, from the outset, its purpose is to be a person. I had no idea what I would become as a child. I grew, like everyone, into my life one choice at a time. A fractured worldview, one without a belief in God, provides no means to grow into a faithful individual or shape a healthy society. Communism, like paganism, keeps society rehearsing and acting out the same old failures and myths over and over again. It maintains the same alliances with fear and power. The government's job, under these conditions, is to try its best to maintain order over the resultant chaos. The nature of political or cultural power, in many governments, is capricious because it's determined not by Gospel principles, but the whim of those who have secured power's privileges. The most egregious crimes against humanity have been perpetrated by those who are willing to go to any lengths to maintain their death grip on the opiate of power's control, with hatred, fear, and violence. Examples of individual and political nihilism are abortion, violence, euthanasia, and the weaponizing of political and economic power.

Fetal euthanasia kills not only the baby, but the conscience of the mother, and the cohesion of community. It separates us from the recognition, and affirmation, of the new creation. There is no greater blight on the conscience of society and the nation as the willful termination of its future. Those who justify the procedure (I am not speaking here about a tubal pregnancy or double-effect cases) do so at the peril of their own human value. Once life is understood as optional, whether in its infancy or in its old age, then between these polarities life is also threatened. If we can abort our past and our future, there is no hope for the present. Any government policy that supports this practice, any organization that stands behind it, any institution that condones it, anyone who participates in it is providing a safe harbor to death and societal destruction. The construction of false arguments that attempt to justify it tears deeply at the heart of caring for others. I am convinced that the anger we see today in society and the fractures in family life can be traced back to *Roe v. Wade*. When the justice system provides safeguards to this kind of violence, then the justice system becomes a means to threaten everyone. The new creation is assaulted, and the territory of fear and destruction is promoted in an attempt to darken God's glory (John Paul II, 1995).

How do we stand against this and other attacks on Christ and the new creation? Considering how this battle is shaping up, it's vital that we use God's resources and His power to sustain our witness to Jesus's victory over sin and death. The principles that I have outlined—living in divine providence, living in creativity, living in generosity, living in reciprocity, living in authenticity, living in unity, living in reconciliation, and living in the Beatitudes—are patterns the Holy Spirit teaches and mature in our hearts us as we freely choose to love Jesus and live in the new creation.

The Word of God suggests that the farther humanity wandered from the Garden of Eden, the shorter was its life expectancy. The Old Testament points out that when Abraham and Sarah conceived a child in their old age, it was a sign of God's intervention. When Elizabeth, Mary's cousin, conceived in her old age, again it was a miracle. The new creation of God's plan of redemption introduced a connection back to that original garden, when age was no problem, because there was no death. God's interventions both legitimized His purposes and point us to the new creation. Mary's conception of Jesus was outside the patterns of human fecundity but was ripe with the fruit of the new creation (Lk. 1:26–45).

Our culture today is fixated on death, because we are so afraid of it. Just channel surf any evening, and you can witness hundreds of murders and acts of violence being acted out on television. There seems to be no solution to the decay of society. Even though science and medicine take credit for making the average life expectancy go up and up. Recently, because of an aging population and narcotic addiction among young people causing overdoses and deaths, the life expectancy has dropped (CDC, 0.1). The scientific model cannot make life meaningful, beautiful, productive, and heroic. The effects of medical advancements, for many, only mean that they are sicker longer. It seems that the more we chase after a secular, atheistic or agnostic solution, by catering to our fear of death without God, the more society crumbles under the weight of disbelief, dissatisfaction, and drug addiction and self-destruction.

The Fruit of Living in the New Creation

Living in the principles of the new creation produces something. St. Paul mentions the benefits of this experience in Galatians 5:22–26, which says, "But the Spirit produces love, joy, peace, patience, kindness, goodness, faithfulness, humility, and self-control. There is no law against such things as these."

The fruit of being grafted into the vine of God are graced virtues. The Holy Spirit produces these virtues in the heart of the person. The seed of the Spirit is sown, watered, and fed in our hearts (John. 16 ff). The results of the new creation can be seen and tested. The good fruit that St. Paul describes is recognizable because it yields good decisions and leads to good outcomes. Moral and ethical choices that stem from the principles in the Word of God generate fruits that are congruent with their nature. That's why Jesus says, "Apart from me you can do nothing" (John 15:5). Outside the envelope of the person of Jesus, there is no safeguard that moral choices will be conceived in goodness to mature and produce good fruit. Just the opposite is more likely choices that are made without Jesus would produce something that is tainted by human pride, self-interest, and arrogance.

My wife made the best apple pie. Every so often, she would make one for me. It was my favorite. She had decided to make me an apple pie for Father's Day. She sent me to the store to get some oil, which was the only ingredient that she needed. So, I gladly went, looking forward to this special treat. Well, she made it and put it in the oven. After it had been in there a while, she said, "You know, honey, it smells like pizza in the kitchen." I went in, and sure enough, it smelled like pizza. She looked at me and said, "What kind of oil did you get?"

I replied, "Olive oil like you wanted." We both looked at each other and went to the pantry and found the container of oil that I bought. It had "OLIVE OIL" in big letters on the label, and under the name in small letters was "with garlic." Let me tell you that apples and pizza dough do not belong together. I know from experience. It looked like an apple pie, but it didn't taste or smell like one. The problem is in the ingredients that are used to make the pie. If they are missing or excessive, the failure becomes obvious when it's smelled or tasted. In the same way, decisions that don't include Jesus will confect together a less-than-savory outcome. The consideration of moral issues without Jesus causes a variety of conflicted options and fractured values. They often contradict "living in the principles" that I have described.

In my career as a hospital chaplain, I have participated and chaired many biomedical ethics meetings. The purpose of the ethics committees is to make recommendations about what decisions would be in the patient's best interest for their healthcare, if there is no recognized surrogate, because for some reason the patient is "unable" (incompetent) to decide for themselves. The committee also is a resource for medical professionals and caregivers and families. It's most often concerned about withdrawal of life support and questions about consent and issues dealing with end-of-life decisions. The principles that are used by most commonly used by committees are "patient autonomy, non-maleficence, beneficence, and justice"(DeGrazia, et al., 2011, 7^{th}ed). These four principles are applied to each case. Bio-medical ethics committees don't identify the most significant principle of all, namely, "Jesus," because most secular ethical systems hang on human philosophy and not on Christian theology. Religion is often viewed as a hurdle that has to be climbed over, or around, to avoid belief's cumbersome pitfalls. Medical professionals can regard theology as an ingredient that doesn't mix well with the outcomes of secular science or situation ethics, hedonism, existentialism, or political philosophies, such as feminism, environmentalism, or socialism. The result of discounting religious values in moral or ethical decisions excludes the fundamental reasons upon which those choices are made. These imposed "secular" limits place belief on a remote street outside the building of real human concern. Religion, for many, should be considered only at the request of the patient or family. Those living in the new creation know that without the cornerstone the building stands upon, it will collapse out of human folly. There is no substitute for the love of Jesus and no way around Him to an alternate set of values (Luke 6:46–49). All goodness resides in Him. Hospital ethics committees make recommendations from a secular point of view. I bring with me the worldview of Jesus as a counterweight of faith into the cases that are discussed. It's my calling, as a chaplain, to carry Christ's worldview into the medical arena and not to apologize for it or allow its importance to be dismissed.

In most studies, there is a control that does not change, whose value is well known and constant. The control is called a "placebo." Even though the medicine is only a sugar pill, because the participant has received something they think is medication, some of the time they feel better (called the placebo effect). The placebo has no medical reason to make the person well. Because this "placebo effect" has been identified and measured, it can be counted on and, according to the NIH, must be factored into any research project.

I went to Washington several years ago, because our ministry wanted to get a grant to study the effect of pastoral care on patients' health. There were people who had come from all over the United States to meet with a man who was an expert in the "placebo effect." All the people who came to the meeting were experts in their fields. They were social and medical scientists who were working on projects that were all seeking funding from the National Institutes of Health (NIH). A study of any merit had to include this model. I was amazed that there was a person whose whole career was centered just about this "effect." Yet for any research project, the "effect" has to be factored in. Without it, the study is regarded as "second rate" and would likely not be approved by the NIH.

Living in the new creation has a "constant." His name is Jesus Christ. It's not an "effect" that works a small percentage of the time. He is the center of all that is good. Jesus and the new creation, communicated by the Holy Spirit, are the "constant" revelation of the will of the Father. God's plan of salvation and redemption is revealed all around us. God's creative energy sparks all matter into existence. It spreads out the universe and places us in its design and wonder. He is the constant presence of God tying all matter and space within the mantle of the Father's ongoing creation. Christ's redemption draws all things to Him. Paul's letter to the Ephesians says it this way,

"God put all things under Christ's feet and gave him to the church as supreme Lord over all things. The church is Christ's body, the completion of him who himself completes all things everywhere" (Eph. 1:22–23). Living in the new creation of Jesus Christ produces the same qualities of trust and obedience to God's will as Jesus has in the Scriptures. The benefits that we see in the life of Jesus, revealed to us in the Gospels, celebrate the new creation on every page. The freedom to make good choices that reveal the love of God resides in His Son. There is no higher calling, no greater vocation, no more perfect freedom than to love Jesus and to live in the Holy Spirit.

> I came upon my friend's silhouette, light against the dark.
> Closer, ever closer, I approached…reaching out my arms.
> I saw the love in your smile that lit up my heart,
> and cried a mystic song, "My beloved, there you are!"

Chapter 14

Living in the Body of Christ

The title for this chapter may seem odd. We don't often speak about ourselves or the church this way. We tend to relate to one another as individuals on our own spiritual journey and the church as an outside or separate institution. I have discussed at some length about living within the context of Christ's redemption and salvation, but now comes the hard part. What does it mean to be a believer and live in community? What's so great about community anyway? My experience as a chaplain has taught me that most people either have dropped out of church or have never or rarely attended a church. The number of those who have left the church seems to be growing with every successive generation (Pew foundation U. S. statistics). My concern is that America is moving closer and closer to a worldview that leaves religion to little old ladies and darkened churches. Like Europe, people may go to see the art or architecture or even hear a concert from a bygone era, but nothing really more than that. The church could be consigned to a historical appendage that culture will validate as a nice memory of a simpler age because it was incapable of keeping up with the pace of societal evolution and technology. The critique of the church as irrelevant is very difficult to deal with. The Christian community sometime seems to unconsciously confirm this notion. The church may be content to huddle around its small campfire of truth and doctrine. It tries, the best it can, to contain what little heat it has against a harsh, cold, and encroaching godless worldview.

Paul gives us an entirely different way of thinking about who we are. Paul draws from the Gospel the precise antidote to the collapse of religion, "the body of Christ." The fabric of society is held together by the bonds of common law, family relationships, benefits of culture, and a myriad of mutual concerns and values. Layer upon layer of political, economic, and educational connections create the web of modern civilization. When we ask the question where does religion fit in all these building blocks of post-modern reality, the answer seems to be more and more "outside the city wall of concern or importance." Paul opens the gate of this "city of resistance" to the entrance of a new king. Jesus's entrance into Jerusalem in the Gospels tells us that he arrives not to tear down, but to redeem and save. He comes riding on a donkey, not in power or splendor, but a humble "Messiah" with the open hand of love and care (Luke 19:28–40).

Jesus sets the church in motion by selecting not perfect people, but flawed ones. The Gospels don't hide the limitations and personalities of the apostles by trying to create a myth of perfection. They expose them for everyone to read and ponder. The disciples are not demigods or elites; they are people just like us. They are moved by God's grace, and the Holy Spirit, to maintain a commitment to the Gospel and to their primitive Christian communities. The early church symbol of an anchor reminds us of the necessity of being grounded in Jesus Christ. He is the safe harbor in the storms of cultural upheaval and social change. Civilizations have come and gone; empires have emerged and disappeared. There have been wars and famines, yet the church has somehow endured it all. The most difficult element of our faith is not belief in Christ, but the belief in the importance of community. It's the place where we can be hurt the most. It's the place where we can feel very vulnerable. It's the place where we can be affirmed and nurtured or ignored, betrayed, and disappointed.

St. Paul moves us away from defining the church by a purely institutional model to a new paradigm of the body of Christ and the new creation. He draws us into the idea that the community of faith is interconnected and functions as the person who is its pattern of existence. The hub of meaning, value, caring, and ministry revolves around the person of Jesus. Without the control of this constant center of gravity, community tends to veer off course. It begins to meet its own needs at the expense of the poor, the brokenhearted, and the people it's called to serve. Acting in unity, as the body does for every task or function, is the by-product of being in the body of Christ (1 Cor. 12:12–29). When Paul says that "we are the body of Christ," it's no longer just a metaphor, a nice way to explain a difficult concept. The body of Christ is not "like" something else. When you are in the body of Christ, you are alive in every way, you are graced in every way, and all the things that the person may be going through, both good or bad, success or failures, sufferings or joys and pleasures, have a purpose and meaning, because Jesus Christ is in it all, and we are His body (Eph. 4:1–16).

My experience of conducting thousands of patient interviews tells me that people give up on the church far too easily. When a painful cluster of events comes calling, we pitch the church out the window. It becomes a painful reminder of the loss or hurt or fear that overwhelmed our ability to cope with life's painful human realities. Giving up on the church is the kind of disengagement that has consequences to our ability to follow Jesus.

We see Jesus walking straight through the resistance of the religious authorities to His message. Yet, Jesus does not retaliate against anyone who even abandons the community or lives outside it, even though He stays faithful to its highest principles. He goes out, as a good shepherd, to find the lost sheep and carry it home (Jn. 10:11–19).

The first place we find the church is right where we live and work. Each person is a church; they are the body of Christ. I believe we must start at the basic truth, "love one another as I love you." The categorical imperative and the principles that spring from it are the foundation for anyone who claims to be living in Christ (Jn. 15:12).

Years ago, Dorothy and I and the kids were living in Austin, Texas. I had just finished a year of seminary. It had been a wonderful experience. I had completed a unit of clinical pastoral education at Austin State Hospital and theological study. I needed to find work. A pastor from a church in the hill country of Texas heard about me somehow, and we talked. He hired me to be his assistant at his congregation. A couple of years went by, and we mostly got along with each other. The time for the annual meeting came up; and to my surprise, at the meeting, it was noted by several members that I needed a raise in salary. The recommendation was made and unanimously adopted. It was quite a substantial increase in my pay. The rector didn't get a raise at all. My heart sank, because I knew that the pastor would not be happy about that decision of the congregation. I was right. As soon as I went over to the parish office, the rector was waiting for me and fired me on the spot. We had just purchased a house, and we had no savings, and now I had no job. I called the senior warden of the congregation to see if anything could be done. He said that he was powerless to help because the assistant pastor worked completely at the pastor's discretion. He would, however, call the bishop and recommend me and discuss the situation. The bishop called and informed me that there was only one mission that needed a vicar and asked if I would be willing to go there. I had no options if I wanted to serve the diocese. So Dorothy and I and the kids packed up our car, a U-Haul truck, rented out our house, and moved. It began a history of transitions that eventually led to my founding PCA, our hospital chaplaincy program. Looking back on this time in our lives, it was one of trial and suffering. Many people would have tossed in the towel and left the ministry. We kept our focus on God's divine providence, trusting that out of sorrow and pain, God would create a new future.

Being in the ministry of service to "Christ's body" does not mean that everything will be easy or fine. The sufferings Jesus endured will be consonant in the Holy Spirit so that your life will be like His. Vocations are watered by the pain of the church being less than what it should be, both in its ministers and in the community. Living in the new creation is believing that when pain and sufferings happen, we live in the hope of that day when the bride of the Christ, His body the church, will be fully clothed in glory and splendor. The belief in Jesus, and the new creation when life is difficult, puts us in touch with the day of fulfillment right now.

Denominations tend to be concerned with jurisdictional, organizational, and doctrinal purity. Throughout the history of the church, it has stood up against false teaching and cultural confusion. Paul's letters were written to address both moral and doctrinal questions that arose in the Christian communities he founded. Paul is very determined that they should "follow the Gospel that he preached" (Gal. 1:6–10). It's easy to understand, going back to the early church, why there can be a mentality of defensiveness over the beliefs and polity of one group over and against another. Sometimes its ministers are treated poorly by the very people it wishes to serve. Sometimes the pastor's own failures to live the Gospel by word and example can bring hurt and pain to the body of Christ. We can choose, however, to rededicate ourselves to live in the experience of faith and hope in the new creation "now" in Christ. We can endure being misunderstood or facing our own failures, because we are blessed to stand on the side of the Father's worldview of redemption and to bring that day closer to its complete fulfillment, because through Jesus and in the Spirit, it has arrived in us.

St. Paul says it this way, "Through the Son, then, God decided to bring the whole universe back to Himself. God made peace through his Son's sacrificial death on the cross and so brought back to himself all things, both on earth and in Heaven" (Rom. 8:1–4).

"At one time you were far away from God and were his enemies because of the evil things you did and thought. But now, by means of the physical death of his Son. God has made you his friends, in order to bring you, holy, pure, and faultless, into his presence. You must of course, continue faithful on a firm and sure foundation, and must not allow yourselves to be shaken from the hope you gained when you heard the gospel. It is of this gospel that I, Paul, became a servant—this gospel which has been preached to everybody in the world" (Col. 1:15–23).

It's a simple truth that when a person is in pain, whether spiritual, emotional, or physical, they tend to do, or say, painful things. We are not meant to live in the unconscious painful darkness of distrust, fear, or judgment. We live in the new creation, which means to be healed, forgiven, and renewed in the Holy Spirit. Good moral and ethical choices reside in the heart of each believer. As parts of Christ's body, like St. Paul, we share in its benefits and its difficulties and sufferings (2 Cor. 7–16). There really is no place to run from community, because we are a new creation in Jesus. There's no excuse that puts us outside the boat of the church if we are a believer. There is no option that the culture promotes that sanctions a private religion. We are part of Christ's body, and because we are His, we are His church (Matt. 26:17–30).

Living in the body of Christ means to be perfected by living in communion with the Father through Jesus and empowered in the new creation by the Holy Spirit. At the same time, it means being part of His body, the church. The communion of these two things makes one thing clear: faith in Christ Jesus is not a private matter. There is no way around community. Belief in Jesus is living in the Body of Christ (Jn. 17:20–25).

> A safety net of your loving care enveloped me.
> I did not try to escape—captured in my wounded snare.
> Satisfied that I was no prisoner, but finally free,
> exhausted by my struggle, my resistance disappeared.

Chapter 15

Living in the Virtues of Caring

I touched on the importance of caring before in this book and placed it as a principle within the Gospel. It's also a fruit of living in all the other principles. Virtues have a quality about them that is both a transcendent gift and a hands-on response to a person's need. Living in the new creation moves us in the Spirit, to get involved in ministry, by caring for others, which is service to the body of Christ.

My wife, Dorothy, died five years ago of Parkinson's. It's difficult to be a caregiver. It wasn't just because of the work or the stress or even the worry. It was, for me, the pain of being so intimately connected to the suffering and unable to make is stop, or even bring relief. A year before Dorothy died, she had been in the hospital for a week or so, and I decided that I wanted to read her medical record. After all, I thought to myself, *I am a hospital chaplain and her husband.* So, I went behind the nurses' station and pulled her chart. I sat down and began to read the doctor's note on her present condition. It said something that shook me. I remember sitting back in the chair and looking up to heaven and saying to myself, "Oh no no." It started off with "This is a seventy-year-old female who has end-stage Parkinson's disease." No one had ever told me, not my doctor friends, or the nurses I worked with, or even the medical professionals whom I trusted and relied on, that her condition was "end stage." It's a tough thing to see a person you love slowly lose their battle for life. Dorothy had been hospitalized many times and had always come back, although each recovery was an incremental retreat. We both held on to each other, even if it meant that there was less and less of her. I knew from my years of ministry to the sick and dying that "end stage" meant a year or less to live. I was so inside the bubble of caring that I was completely taken by surprise. Why had nobody told me? Why had they not taken me aside and conveyed openly the facts that I discovered? It was like one of those ugly secrets that everybody else knew but me. Was I blind for not seeing the obvious, or were they just afraid of having that conversation? Or was I too afraid? Doing the tasks of making all the doctors' appointments, bathing, pill times, feeding, and caring for someone who is chronically ill, often the caregiver loses perspective of what's really happening. I had defined my world around hers, and that world was slipping away, and someday soon, it would be gone forever. There it was, in black and white, written in stone with pen, like Job (19:23–25).

After I had received reality's cold, wet towel in my face, the question became what to do? We had been married for thirty-four years, and we had a wonderful relationship. It's not to say that we never fought or had disagreements; of course, we did. I know that somehow; I became instantly committed to the idea that as long as we had time together, I would not say "no" to her. If she said she wanted to do something or said she wanted something, I would do my best to provide it. Her life would be hard enough, and whatever she needed or wanted, I was determined to give her. Dorothy was not hard to please, but she had special things she liked to do. Going shopping at the mall was the first item on her list, followed by going to Hobby Lobby to get stickers for her letters and getting her hair and nails done with regularity. She was every bit a woman and loved being feminine and maternal. She considered herself everyone's mother, even me sometimes when no one else was around.

The next thing I did was to cut back on my work as much as I could. I stopped teaching biomedical ethics at the college. I still had to work at the hospital, but I got chaplains to cover when I needed extra time with her. These two things were the best decisions I made during her illness. She was not a complainer. Dorothy was always a partner with me in the ministry. I felt her relax with this new rhythm. She seemed happier and more content. We grew closer in a different kind of way to one another, by giving and receiving care from each other. I mention receiving, because I benefited from her affirmation as she often told me how blessed she was to be married to me. How wonderful a husband I was. How she had a life that was full of love and that it was never dull. Care-giving softens a person's heart by giving and receiving. It does not diminish a person or rob them of their energy. Care taking has the opposite effect; it just makes our hearts hardened by the duties and demands and all the difficult tasks and burdens.

People would ask me, "How do you do it all? They would also say, "Don't forget to take time for yourself." As if I needed some advice to manage things better. In the bubble of caregiving, there isn't time or energy to get outside it. It's like a goldfish swimming around in a small bowl. Everything is somehow contained in it, and the fish can survive. All the fish understands is living in that small space. It's all the fish knows, and for a time, it's all that the fish has or needs. Dorothy and I were both swimming around in the aquarium of suffering. It was what we knew, and it limited our world to a smaller and smaller portion of mobility, of physical and emotional choices. Yet God provided more and more of His grace. His Spirit made it possible for me to keep all our ministries going and even growing. We never faltered, because we were not alone. We had the people of God and Jesus to accompany us. I could do it all because we were living in the new creation. When I look back into those years, and especially the last one of her life, caring for her didn't wear me out or overwhelmed me, because we were swimming in the ocean of the new creation. Where others see the limitation of a small container of suffering, Jesus lives in the ocean of God's glory and shares it with us. In these moments or hours or days or weeks or even years of caregiving, a wonderful thing takes place. Jesus makes the burden light so that we can endure the yoke of hardship (Matt. 11:28–30).

It happened in a very short space, within forty-eight hours, a year later, that her life that was so precious to her, and to me, slipped outside her skin and soared into glory, leaving me behind. Our time together became a past tense and silence has been a more constant companion ever since. I deeply miss her. Sometimes I wonder if I bore people by singing our romantic stories over and over again—the lyrics of our life together and the risks we took in being one. There is, however, another thing that touches my heart when I think of her, not just her perfume or smile or the way she said my name; it's all those things and more. It was all wrapped up in the way she cared for me and I for her. She left behind for me the love of Jesus, a man well acquainted with grief, as Isaiah says (Is. 53:3). We sit down together in prayer, and I tell Him about her, and He brings her back to life in my memory. I will always have the love and caring we shared. Jesus has met me in my grief. He carried my wounds on His back and fixed my sin to the tree of forgiveness. He has washed me in the nature of His caring so that I can care for others.

Union with God means communion with His love and caring for others. If we live in the caring heart of Jesus, then the new creation is open to us. The Holy Spirit leads us, and we have fellowship with the Father. Jesus speaks of this communion in John 6:35–36: "I am the bread of life, He who comes to me will never be hungry. He who believes in me will never be thirsty." We experience divine communion with God by coming to Jesus, which means running into His arms. It's not a begrudging acknowledgment that in the end, He has ultimate power and control. Our coming to Jesus is like a child who is thrilled by our Father's return. It's a celebration that claims the prize of our wholehearted sense of belonging to God. Coming to Jesus is not looking over our shoulder for a better offer that is tempered by "maybes" or "we'll sees." So many people reserve the right to themselves to carefully dole out belief only when they have been totally convinced and when it works in their favor. Coming to Jesus is a recognition that wherever we find Him, we run to care. We will never be hungry because His love fills up our plate with more to do and accomplish. Jesus satisfies our hunger from the things we think "we need" to what He gives that fills us up with good things. The person who comes to Him trusts that God's storehouse of blessings in the new creation is available to them. Making good choices using the principles that we have discussed shreds the culture's mythic gods, because they can't fill a person up with meaning. Those myths lead people to be so self-absorbed that they run over anyone who gets in their way and become blind to the needs of others. Coming to Jesus is not an escape, or an exit, to some "higher power." Coming to Jesus is a way of life that invites personal growth through caring for one another as Christ cares for us.

Deprivation/Restoration and the New Creation

We become aware of our hunger, or thirst, because they're present when there is a deprivation. Food and water are necessary to sustain life. Our bodies have a physical reaction when there is a need for replenishment. It becomes more and more urgent the longer food or water is deprived. Every person knows something about hunger and thirst, because at one time or another, we've all experienced it. The way we satisfy our need for food and water, shelter, and the resources for survival has affected not just each person but societies, nations, and the world's economy. The Scriptures indicate, however, that there are other kinds of deprivations and different forms of hunger and thirst. When I am thirsty, my body knows. Being out on a hot summer day in Phoenix will cause a person to sweat and their mouth and lips to dry out. There are other physical symptoms, as the need for hydration becomes more pronounced. The mind and the body can be affected very quickly. I can live longer without food, but my body also signals me with stomach discomfort and muscle weakness. The hunger and thirst in the human spirit can be equally great but hard to recognize. Living in an environment of fear, violence, and conflict can produce physical and mental symptoms. Human caring, compassion, understanding, love, and trust are necessary garments for clothing our spirit. If these are absent, then their deprivation in a person's character can produce a chilling nakedness. We have all been born into a world of deprivation because we are all dealing with the sins of others and our own failures. Jesus was born into our human condition and knows, from His own desert experience, what it means to be without food or water. We are told that the Spirit led Him into this physical deprivation that He overcame by speaking the Word of God to it (Lk. 4:1–13). The new Adam can address the dry places in our hearts. He enters the desert in all of us, where we thirst for truth, freedom, love, and belonging. He enters our hunger for community, for a bright future, for meaning, and for self-worth. He knows all too well the deprivations we all struggle with, especially grief and loss. He brings to our parched and vacant land the living water of the new creation (Jn. 4:1–26). In this land, springs of the Spirit bubble up inside us. Bread, fish and water and wine are multiplied to feed our dreams for the future with hope (Mk. 6:30–43) & (Jn. 2:1–12). We are led to green meadows and abundant pastures by the Good Shepherd, and we are welcomed home to the New Jerusalem (Rev. 21:9–27).

Caring for one another in Christ is the conduit of the new creation. It brings with it the energy and healing of the Father's redemptive work through each person. Caring in Christ produces resources and ministers to people who desperately need these benefits to satisfy their hunger and thirst. Churches, just like people, can be care taking or caregiving places. I want to be part of a caregiving community.

I have worked in hospitals for many years. Some illnesses require that water or food be withheld for the patient's good. The person's condition makes giving these things more painful and even dangerous. I've had patients beg me for water, when I have visited them, or tell me that they haven't eaten in several days and how hungry they are. Healing often requires a deprivation with the goal of restoration. The patient has to accept being in short-term suffering, with the purpose of recovery. The name, PATIENT, is an acknowledgment that the person should be willing to endure the deprivations that come with curing their sickness. The purpose of this stress is not to increase the patient's suffering but to get them well. It's easy to know this from outside the person's pain; it's much harder to go through the process yourself. Visiting a patient in this condition puts the pastoral caregiver in touch with their own deprivations. It's no wonder that often friends and family members avoid the hospital. A pastoral caregiver has to be willing to walk into their own history of pain or suffering and loss. The focus, however, cannot be on the deprivation, but on the restoration side of God's grace. If we are living in the new creation, then we stay with the patient's experience, listening, caring, and praying with and for them. We don't block them with our past experience of pain but use it to enable us, in the Spirit, to appreciate and empathize with the patient's experience and to bring Christ's love to their needs (Savage, 1996).

Living in caring brings a different set of principles to biomedical ethics discussions involved in end-of-life issues. A patient who has placed their hope in the culture's values and myths will be sadly disappointed in its ability to maintain a person's life forever. The attachment to this fantasy promotes a desperate denial when end-of-life care becomes inevitable. Moreover, the human propensity to protect ourselves from painful realities adds another layer to the already-tilted scale of denials and blames. I can't tell you how often I have visited patients in the hospital who have chronic conditions that they have lived with for a long time and have never even thought about filling out an advanced directive (living will and medical power of attorney). Living in the new creation doesn't deny the reality of our human mortality. It's not just a simple recognition of human frailty but celebrates life in the context of its complete emancipation. Paul says, "What we see now is like a dim image in a mirror; then we shall see face to face" (1 Cor. 13:12). There is a new blueprint revealed in Christ and in the new creation. Paul points to this when he says, "Where, Death is your victory? Where, Death is your power to hurt? Death gets its power to hurt from the Law. But thanks be to God who gives us the victory through our Lord Jesus Christ" (1 Cor. 15:55–58).

A Christian who is living in the new creation does not desperately grasp onto the tiniest thread of life, when it's clear that the fullness of the new creation is calling us home to life's sacred fulfillment. They grasp onto Jesus who is life. They take the hand with Him who beckons them into the eternal garden of glory and are prepared to leave behind the repository of the old creation (Jn.14:3–8).

I have attended many ethics consults in the hospital. They use the philosophical principles of autonomy, beneficence, non-maleficence, and justice and apply them in each case. When we put together the interest of the patient and/or surrogate, the interests of the medical staff, the doctor, the family, and the state, these issues can be quite complex. Many people understand life differently and have varied needs and expectations and hoped for outcomes. When you add grief and the apparent failure of the medical model to make the patient well, making health care decisions can be very difficult. If a person is gravely ill and has no family, or surrogate, then the ethics committee can usually come up with "recommendations" rather quickly. I can list for you case after case when these principles are in conflict. There are some cases found in "Biomedical Ethics" a book by DeGrazia, Mappes and Ballard. Ethics cases are sometimes more problematic the more and more people, family members, other interested parties become involved. The worldview of our culture, its laws, and its values often produce a process that looks through a very dark lens indeed. It has to balance resources, competing priorities, rules, and cultural principles that don't often play well together. The reason for this "tied-in-knots reality" is it represents a worldview that's not fundamentally Christian. It can't advocate for the new creation because Christ is not its center of gravity. Occasionally these two can briefly touch, but they will inevitably diverge from one another. I have been asked, "what purpose does a chaplain serve in these discussions?" My experience tells me that a chaplain brings to the "biomedical ethics" conversation a Christian worldview that counters the desert of ethical relativism, hedonism, and situational ethics. Jesus interacted with the culture of His day and proclaimed the new creation. John's Gospel is resplendent with this conversation. Even though the spiritual language of Jesus is unusual and He is misunderstood by almost everyone, including the disciples, Jesus continues to describe His relationship with the Father. He is accused of blasphemy, being in league with the devil, and lawlessness (Jn. 11:14–26). John's Gospel chapter 17:1–25 brings the whole new pattern of God's redemption into clear focus: "We are to be one with Jesus just as He is one with the Father." Not only that, but we are to be one together in Him. This pushes us over the edge of the culture's values and dominance. Still, knowing the conflict His message will bring, He speaks it anyway. My point of view as a chaplain may not be understood or even appreciated but being present in Christ brings the new creation to the complexity and confusion of moral and ethical decision-making. It has been my observation that if the patient, or their surrogate, holds a Christian worldview, there are fewer ethical conflicts over end-of-life decisions. The opposite is true for those with no or little faith or those whose religion is tied to alternate beliefs.

The Law's requirements and legal remedies rarely settles anything on the inside of a person. It has the power to convict, to punish, to control, to maintain order; but the law does not change a person or grace them with meaning or purpose. They may even win the lawsuit and yet still believe they were not treated fairly. The law does not create or make a person new; only the new Adam can do that. Living under the old law puts us under its constraints (Medicare and health insurance rules and guidelines, medical malpractice lawsuits, and hospital policies are just a few examples), and because so many people live under the law, we tend to use its values as the truth. The law's influence is translated by culture and mythic science as a justification for active euthanasia, abortion, and assisted suicide. Once the laws are made that say these are okay (Oregon, Vermont and Washington have laws that support assisted suicide) then there is no civil constraint from defending and using these forms of destruction. Laws can be made that pander to the needs of the powerful, the elite, and those endowed with wealth. These priorities will not birth the new creation. Only Jesus can deliver tomorrow because only He "makes all things New"(Col. 1:15–20).

> Oh, the joy of this reunion, coming home.
> A vagabond, a wayward soul, with no place left to go…
> Right into your embrace, warm, forgiven, and atoned,
> recreated, in the image of my wounded Lord!

Chapter 16

Living in Truth

Telling the truth is the most important element of living in the new creation. Jesus says that "I am the way the truth and the life" (John 14:6). One of the things that strikes me in John's Gospel is how often Jesus says, "I am telling you the truth." It's as if He knows that the things we believe about others, ourselves, and God are so confused that we don't know the truth when it's standing right in front of us. He has to preface his teaching with this important phrase. The Father's truth is a person, Jesus, who stands up for it all the time. He remains steadfast in His relationship with the Father when other threaten Him or challenge Him or when the religious authorities condemn Him. He stays in the truth of His Father's love no matter what may be required to defend it.

Like living in caring, living in truth requires the activation of all the other principles that I have described. The Scriptures give us some simple principles on truth telling, for example. "Say 'Yes' or 'No'—anything else you may say comes from the Evil One" (Matt. 5:37). Owning up to our failures and sins is so difficult because we like to live in the fantasy of our perfection. Blaming others for our misdeeds or shortcomings is a deflection from our responsibility and self-awareness. Getting caught in a lie or a pretense discloses our folly and vulnerability.

I like to play golf. There was a time in my life when I counted all the strokes, good or bad, and carefully kept my score. I played in tournaments where the rules were strictly enforced and compliance expected. It was important to clearly know what my correct score was or face disqualification. My score also defined how good a player I was on any given day. I have to confess that it's quite humbling to admit that the player I thought I was often did not match up with the numbers on my scorecard. I realize that the pros on the Tour have to maintain their edge in scoring to win tournaments and money. Sometimes an amateur player can expect their game to be on par with those who practice and play for a living. When I played, I found myself often getting very frustrated with my score and beginning to enjoy the game less and less. Then one day, as I was heading off to the course for another round of self-criticism, it hit me: *Michael, you're never going to be a pro player, nor do you want to be. The best you can hope for is to enjoy the game. Just think, you're out with nature, the grass, the sunshine, the exercise, and the pleasure of the day. What if I didn't keep score? What if I simply played golf without the pressure of performance? I'm not playing in a tournament. I'm out to be with nature and to have the joy of the experience, whether I hit a good shot or a bad one.* I finally figured out how to play golf. If there's no one playing with me, and that's often the case in Phoenix in the summer, I hit an extra ball or two and work on my game. If I'm playing with someone or a foursome, sometimes people ask me what I got on that last hole. I simply tell them, "I don't keep score." They look at me with a certain disbelief. Sometimes people I'm playing with will invite me to bet on a hole or a round. I say, "Well, I guess I could do that, but I don't keep score, so I don't bet on my game." I have discovered something about golf and something about life. Playing the game is its own reward. It's not about the score. It's about the experience. The truth is, I don't keep score outside of a recognition if I played the hole well or not.

The Pharisees were all about keeping score. They had a score to settle with the Romans, the Greeks, and the Samaritans. They kept playing the game by picking winners and losers. They watched Jesus to trip Him up in the religious "sand traps" that they set for Him. They counted their interpretation of the "law" as the official scorecard of righteousness and social acceptance. They bent the rules for themselves but demanded perfection from everyone else. The game they played was only for a few, and it kept others from playing (Matt. 7:6–24).

Hypocrisy shields a person from the truth. It fabricates a world that needs no salvation since I am the final arbiter for what is true or not. Jesus plays the game for the sheer love of the Father and His people. He reveals what it means to live in the truth, not by the law, but in the new creation of grace. He can forgive the woman caught in adultery, stay in a sinner's house, heal on the Sabbath, and upset the money changers tables in the temple. Since Jesus is the truth, everyone can play the game. We can celebrate successes and failures, invite others to play, and trust the scorecard into His hands. Sometimes the course can be challenging, with unexpected twists, turns, and hazards. There's pain and loss, hurt, and fear in life; but if we play the game His way, the course of our life will be full of truth and love.

My most difficult shot should be the easiest. When I'm about ninety to sixty yards from the hole, I tend to try to guide the ball to the target. When I do that, my swing gets out of rhythm, and I usually mishit the shot by hitting behind the ball. This is not a good outcome at all. However, if I focus on the swing and trust the timing and give up the need to control the outcome, and just let the club move freely, the outcome is usually better. Being in relationship to Jesus Christ means giving over to Him control of our life. It requires that we trust Him with the things we want to manipulate and gain advantage for ourselves. It can be family or relationships, work, finances, and our ego. If I try to control others or circumstances or fill my world with my own guided outcomes, then a self-fabricated worldview will inevitably include dishonesty. If I choose to place my life in the Father's care through His Son Jesus and live in the Holy Spirit, the outcome will be the right one, because I'm choosing to live in the truth.

Years ago, I had a friend of mine visit from out of town and stay with us in our home in Glendale. I invited him to come with me to play golf. He told me that he didn't play golf and had no desire to learn. I suggested that he just drive the cart and come along. "The course I play at is like a big park with pine trees and several ponds. Even though you are in the heart of the city, it feels like you're miles away," I told him. Reluctantly he agreed, and off we went. He was quite surprised by the way I played. He asked me, "What did you get on that last hole, so I can write down your score?"

I replied, "I don't keep score. I just play the game."

He laughed and laughed and shook his head and said, "I've never heard of such a thing." As we moved around the course, I played, and he drove the golf cart. He began to tell his story. It seems that his father was quite a good golfer, even better than good. He also was a perfectionist and demanded that if his son was going to play golf, it required a person to keep the rules and play the game as strictly as he did. There was no real fun involved, but a determination to improve and practice as often as you could. My friend saw, as a young person, these expectations as unreasonable demands on his autonomy by a dominating and judgmental parent. He decided never to play golf. As we approached the last few holes, he stopped the cart and looked out at the course and said, "I've had a really great day. If you had told me that I could have fun at a golf course, I would have told you to go jump in that lake over there. If my father had only taught me to play golf the way you do, I would have played this game. It can be fun. I never knew that before."

Hearing the Truth

We tend to build our worldview around the "truths" we hear from others and our own inner voice. We usually react to what we hear, when there is pain, with self-protection because of our needs for safety and autonomy. We can erect a well-fortified defense and guard its ramparts with hyper vigilance and stockpile our hurts behind its walls. We can build a set of life commandments (Savage, 1996) that keep others away. The voice we need to hear is God's Word. Jesus is the truth we seek. There are no walls that He will not scale to save us. There are no defenses that He has not overcome through His death and resurrection. There is no fear that will keep Him out, because His love is a powerful truth. Nothing can overcome Him, not the past, not sin, and not death. The victory of truth, for you and me, hinges on our inviting Him to enter into our life. All we have to do is let down the drawbridge of our heart and welcome in His truth.

There are voices that can wound us with half-truths, by reciting old painful memories, or remind us of the dull edges of our lost hopes and failures. The loudest voice we hear so clearly is our own. What I say to myself about my experience and history can be a toxic soup of rehearsed emotional pain and deprivation. When we listen to only our own voice, we can tune out listening for God's truth. We have "ears to only hear our human voice." Jesus reminds us of this reality in the Gospels when He says, "Listen, then, if you have ears!" (Mark 4:9). Listening to others and listening to God means that a person has an openness to the message another person is sending. It requires us to step outside our own inner dialogue to enter the communication of words, body language, and tone of what the other person. "If we have ears" implies that we let the message of the Gospel penetrate our tightly held personal truths and their defenses to allow God's truth to take root. If we're going to listen to God, then we must be open to the content of His message. Jesus reflects purely what He hears from the Father He's not interested in communicating a message to fit the situation. Rather, He communicates the message that changes the situation with the truth (Jn. 5:19–30)

Nicodemus comes at night to ask Jesus to explain Himself and His teaching (John 3:1–31). He comes seeking a response that will answer his inner conflicts about Jesus. Instead, he gets a message that changes the entire dialogue. Jesus is the one with the questions. He redirects Nicodemus to answer the question of belief. If Nicodemus is to hear, he needs to be listening. He must be willing to have his own inner voice "muted" to allow himself to question his worldview. He has to have "ears to hear." The truth will not help anyone who is not willing to hear it. The Word of God will only activate us if we lend our ears to listen to God's voice. Just as Jesus listens to the Father's voice, in the Scriptures, we listen to Him. We listen to Jesus in the Holy Spirit, who makes His voice known to us (Jn. 14:25–27).

John's Gospel (6:25–59) points out to us that when He tells them that He is the bread of life and that His flesh is real food and His blood is real drink, people begin to grumble against him. Then they begin to leave. It's interesting that before they leave, they grumble, like their ancestors in the desert who grumbled against Moses. They even had a name for it "Marah" (Exod. 15:23–25). Jesus loses their "better ear," and they stop believing and following. They are being taught about a whole "new worldview," like Nicodemus, that doesn't fit into their religious/cultural understanding. The only people left are the apostles, and their response is quite interesting too. When Jesus asks them if they are going to leave as well, they say, "Where shall we go, you have the words of everlasting life" (John 6:68–69). The apostles were willing to let the Father's Word crack the shell of their understanding, their religious traditions, and its legal requirements. They are left with one thing to stand on—that is the truth of God's Word. Jesus is the living Word, the flesh and blood of the truth.

Seeing the Truth

There's a big difference between matzo and bread. There's no yeast in matzo, and as a result, it's like a cracker. It resists molding and takes up little space, because matzo is flat. It's easy to take on a journey because of these characteristics. Matzo, unless you put an herb or other condiment with it, has little real flavor. It's one of the main elements of the Passover meal that the Jews celebrate once a year to remember their flight from Egypt (Exod. 12:8–9). They recall God's deliverance of His people from the hands of the Pharaoh. Bread rises because of the yeast in it and can spoil more quickly. Bread tastes better than matzo. It has a softer texture, is more playable, and is more satisfying. We can see the difference between the two. Matzo is rather two-dimensional; it has no depth. Bread, on the other hand, because it rises, has depth and is three-dimensional.

I like to paint and draw, and I consider myself an artist. I can take a two-dimensional surface and make it appear to the eye as if it's three-dimensional. A good artist can recreate a subject and make it look real and inviting, the same with photography and television. 3D movies can make the film appear so real that you can almost touch the objects in the scene. We know that this is an illusion. The artist uses contrasts, color, and skill to trick the eye to believe that something is three-dimensional when it's really only two.

Jesus speaks about Himself as the "Living Bread come down from heaven." He's not the matzo but the "Living Bread." He provides something that takes us from the two-dimensional world of "sin and death" and brings us into the real three-dimensional world of the new creation. He is the yeast that brings depth and meaning. We can be fooled by the two-dimensional flat existence that provides some sustenance, with little taste, and is filled with our human limitations. The world can be a dangerous place, with suffering, human frailties, pain, and violence. Jesus invites us to "taste and see how good is the Lord" (Psalm 34:8). We see Him in his teaching, describing for us the "spiritual depth" of meaning and the truth of the Father's love. "He can do this because He is the living bread that came down from heaven" (John 6:51).

At the Last Supper, Jesus takes the matzo and adds Himself to it. "This is my body and my blood." It appears to be matzo, but now it's the "bread of life." Seeing the two-dimensional reality of our human nature change requires "spiritual sight." The leaven of Jesus's death and resurrection rises us out of our flat existence. We are called in Jesus to experience the depth of God's love for us and for creation. Communion with Christ means we see Him in each person. We recognize Him in each experience. We acknowledge that receiving Him means we believe that He receives our matzo and raises it up into the new creation. We can see the depth of God's glory in creation and give Him praise and worship. We can see Him even in suffering, our own and others, making His love known. He brings redemption out of sorrow and pain. Because the matzo of our humanity now is raised, we are not fooled by the appearance of the culture of success, power, and self-absorption. Good moral choices are produced by believing that even when things appear flat and tasteless, Jesus is producing meaning and raising up our souls matzo with the leavening of His Father's love in the Spirit. Seeing the truth is a product of being in the Spirit.

We can see Him in community. St. Paul says, "We are the Body of Christ" (1 Cor. 12:27). It's very difficult for people today to recognize the importance of belonging. It seems that building Christian community is easier left till some later date. Paul reminds us that community is not just about being warm and understood but about a commitment to spiritual growth. We belong to the body of Christ because we are the body of Christ. It's easy to say that when we are by ourselves, thinking holy thoughts, until the hardships of our human condition become colored with conflict and different values and contrasting motives. The Gospel draws us back to the central teaching of Jesus, when he says,

"If you love me you will obey my commandments. I will ask the Father, and he will give you another Helper, who will stay with you forever. He is the Spirit, who reveals the truth about God. The world cannot receive him, because it cannot see him or know him. But you know him, because he remains with you and is in you" (John 14:15–18).

Seeing God's new creation requires spiritual sight. The Holy Spirit transmits that vision to see God's work and presence in the world. The Holy Spirit communicates the Father's will, His plan at work in society and in each person (Eph. 1:14). We can discern, through the Spirit, what is good from what is bad. The Father's worldview is projected to us in the Holy Spirit. Belief in Jesus is a grace that comes through the Spirit, and every good and honorable act comes from the storehouse of the goodness and love of the Holy Spirit. Even the motivation to do good is conducted by the Holy Spirit, because goodness is a spiritual gift (1 Cor. 12:1–11).

I have had a long career of ministry in the church with failures and even a few successes. Looking back at what God blessed, I am humbly aware that the Holy Spirit was the facilitator for anything good that was accomplished. If we want to know the truth, we must see it in the Holy Spirit.

When I visit a patient, there's a lot to observe: their physical condition, the restrictions on the door for isolation, their ability to communicate verbally, the amounts of drips, whether they are on the ventilator or not. The next thing I observe is, are there get-well cards or balloons or flowers? These realities frame a picture of what the patient may be going through. Is there anyone with the patient visiting them? What feelings are produced in me as I see the condition of the patient? There is an internal and external environment; seeing the outside often gives us an insight to the internal world of the patient, but not always. The Holy Spirit helps us see that brokenhearted, lonely, or frightened person who is hoping for the "new creation" to break through the frozen past and raise them up to a new warm future. We recognize that Jesus is attuned in the Spirit to see His mission and to recognize the resistance He would encounter. He saw the apostles not just as they were when He called them, but what they would become as they followed Him. Jesus saw them in the Spirit. When the Spirit came down upon Him, at His baptism by John the Baptist (Matt. 3:13–17), Jesus saw the road ahead and followed the Father's will into the desert and later to call the disciples. It requires spiritual insight to recognize the importance of an event to see ourselves and others in the context of those moments of transition or crisis, exultation, and recovery. The birth of a child, dealing with a chronic illness, graduation, marriage, retirement—all these events and more are visually anchored in our memory. We remember and see ourselves and those events not just as our history, but the castle of our identity. We see each other, and we bring with us the collections of all our experiences and what they means to us. Jesus puts it this way to Philip who asks Him, "Lord, show us the Father. That is all we need."

Jesus answered, "For a long time I have been with you all; yet you do not know me, Philip? Whoever has seen me has seen the Father" (John 14:9–10)?

When we have Jesus in our heart, it's not just a recognition that we acknowledge His divinity or His lordship over all things. We get the benefit of the whole person—His memory of the exultation of creation, the incarnation of His life with us, His sufferings, and His resurrection. These are not just theological exercises. They are the man Himself, and He reveals and brings with Him the Father and His experience. The Holy Spirit shows us this meaning, and it becomes our own so that when people see us, they see Jesus. We see Jesus in others too. The view of our redemption, this lens, becomes the way we see the world around us (1 Cor. 12:12).

Feeling the Truth

Most of us realize how quickly our feelings can change. We know that emotion can be very captivating and can confuse and even control us. Emotion is not bad, but placing too much stock on it can make things very difficult. However, with this caveat, feelings are important indicators of truth. We see Jesus affected by what he encounters in His ministry. He is moved by the widow of Nain in Luke 7:11–17. He weeps over Jerusalem (Lk. 13:-35). He is touched by the woman who has suffered with an issue of blood (Mk. 5:25–32). Throughout the Gospel, we are aware of the deep emotional content of healing, freedom from sin, restoration to community, and suffering. There is joy and celebration too. Jesus feeding the five thousand (Lk. 9:10–17) the transfiguration (Mk. 9:2–12), the revelation of the Godhead in His baptism, (Matt. 3:13–17) and, my favorite, the healing of the blind man in John's Gospel (Jn. 9:1–41) touch the emotional content of God's presence. Jesus is not a stoic or divinely engineered robot. He is a flesh and blood man who has feelings and is affected by them. He gets angry when he is witness to the hypocrisy of the religious elite (Lk. 19:45–48). He is surprised when he finds faith in the Roman centurion (Matt. 8:5–13) or the Canaanite woman (Matt. 15:21–28). Jesus responds emotionally to the truth communicated by the human condition. He is not just an observer but interjects the Father's love everywhere He goes. If we are following Jesus, we will kinesthetically experience the truth.

Living in the truth is not some kind of intellectual exercise devoid of emotional content. When we are living in the truth, we recognize, and affirm, the way feelings affect our understanding and our appreciation of any human experience.

Emotional Recognition

St. Paul in Romans 8:16 says, "God's Spirit joins himself to our spirits to declare that we are God's children." He goes on to tell the benefits of this recognition and it's conflict with the world. What we experience in the presence of the truth is a spiritual and emotional connection. It is an affirmation of the rightness of the subject. Some people use the term "a gut reaction." When something is true, we know it spiritually. It reflects in our Spirit the divine nature of God. It causes an emotional response that validates its congruence with God's purposes or His nature. I'm not talking about doing something that is simply pleasurable or self-serving, but the extension, by self-donation, to the cause of good and the service of others.

Years ago, I was serving in the Diocese of West Texas. Every year there was a clergy-and-spouse retreat. In those days, there were no women priests; so the priests, "the men," went to one place and the "women" to another. Our priests' retreat was held at the camp center for the diocese.

It was relatively primitive. The beds were cots, and the cabins were not air-conditioned. On the other hand, the woman's, "spouses," retreat was held at a tennis ranch about eighty miles away. One day we had a free afternoon, and several of us decided to jump in a car and drive up to the tennis ranch and find out how the other half lived and crash their party. We had only enough time to drive up there and spend thirty minutes before we would need to leave and go back to the conference. So off we went. Ninety minutes later, we drove up to this most beautiful place. It had spacious condos with air-conditioning, fully furnished. It was free from mosquitoes and other critters. It was fantastic. We got out of the car, and we tried to find our wives. My friends had no trouble finding their spouses, since they were all together in a recreation room. I couldn't find Dorothy because she wasn't with the other women. Several of my friends said that it would be a shame to miss her after coming all this way. I thought, where would she be? It came to me that she was probably out praying for me. There was an open field, and across there was a little brook that ran through the property. I headed out that way. As I crossed the field, I heard her voice. There she was running toward me yelling, "Michael! Michael!" It was like one of those B movies where the couple run to each other in slow motion with tall grass and butterflies all around. We hugged, kissed, and laughed and laughed. She wasn't surprised; she was excited because she had been waiting for me. She had a feeling that I would pay her a surprise visit. When the conferences ended and we were home, she confided that several women were jealous and complained, and wondered, why their husbands had not paid them an unexpected visit. Emotional recognition of the truth is an internal knowing that is transcendent. Dorothy recognized me and had been waiting with expectation for my visit. It's difficult to explain to someone without the experience. Love produces this inside feeling of safety and trust. These feelings are not conjured up but come from the nature of the relationship and the fruit of goodness that it produces.

Truth, like love, grows in an environment of safety. Without it, even if there is a kernel of truth, it will feel foreign and conflicted. When Jesus went to the temple and saw the money changers, selling and making money at the entrance to His Father's House of Prayer, He had a visceral reaction. The text uses the feeling word of "zeal" that propels Him to overturn their tables and drive them out of the temple (Matt. 21:12–18). This place was not to be a place where the religious culture provides for itself. It's a place that will be raised up because He will be raised up on the third day. His body will be the New Temple, because the most perfect sacrifice was laid down for us. Sin and death were put to flight, and all the money changers of our past human failures were overturned, and a new creation was being brought to life.

Truthful Congruence

When what we hear, feel, and see match up, this is congruence, and it leads us to believe the truthfulness of the subject (Savage, 1996). We see Jesus healing people in the Scriptures and doing the work of the Father. We hear what He says or teaches. We experience how it produces loving or caring feelings that are aligned with God's purposes. In John's Gospel, there is a word to describe this congruence. It's called "abiding" (John 15 ff). The truth resides in the harmony of these three things together. We know that there is incongruence when the words a person says don't match up with how they are behaving or when the emotional intensity is greater or less than what would be appropriate to the situation or experience. We would be unlikely to believe a person who exhibits emotional, visual, or auditory incongruence. Truth is known by its wholeness—its completeness to the subject at hand. It doesn't skirt difficult issues but faces them directly. It spotlights motives and brings light to the darkness of deceit, avoidance, and self-protection. If we can know the truth by its congruence through the senses, it's also true that our actions, decisions, and motives would need to be congruent spiritually. The choices we make flow from the will of the person, in their spirit. Consent to do good and to avoid evil comes from an interior spiritual grace given by God. Any good decision or action would also be congruent with the person of Jesus Christ. He is revealed to us in the Scriptures, in prayer, in the Christian doctrine, in the sacraments, and by the participation in community of the Holy Spirit. For an act or decision to be good, it is, by the nature of the subject, congruent with the transcendent love of God (Ignatius, 2014 edition). Without spiritual transcendence, to complete the hierarchy of values necessary to discern the truth, we could easily be led astray by our limited perceptions. We could believe a thing is good simply by its sensual appeal. Many people live in this house of cards, building their choices on the sandy ground of their perceptions and their humanistic beliefs. The person of Jesus Christ is the complete revelation of the perfect congruence to the Father's love, communicated to us in the Holy Spirit. He is also the "new Adam" that ministers the new creation. Since He is the perfect revelation of the Father's love, He is also the perfect, personal congruence of the Father's holy will (John 17). When an act or decision is good, it is aligned, by its nature, to be in the will of God. Jesus tells us over and over in John's Gospel that He only does the will of the Father and that He only does what He sees the Father doing (John 10:34–39). When an act or decision is not congruent with God's purposes and His nature, because of willful disregard, pride, arrogance, and selfishness, "sin and evil" are the subsequent fruit from the tree of this rebellion. Truth is obscured by deceit. The subsequent effects of simulation create more distrust and fear.

> Bursting colors dancing all around.
> No confusion or doubt, but exaltation.
> I finally had let my guard come down,
> and forever, I am a *new creation*!

Chapter 17

Moral Synchronicity

Union with God is the most important element of producing good fruit. Good decisions are grown by the good earth of redemption and salvation in Jesus. We have tried over and over again by society, by culture, by humanistic means, by science, and by every form of human knowledge to fashion a better world for ourselves. The evidence shows that this methodology has, at best, under-performed. Politicians and social evolutionists keep trying to do the impossible task of wrestling away from God the meaning and purpose of life.

The difficult choices that are confronting us about what is moral and ethical are not just a construct of laws and governmental guidelines. Rules are societal norms of behavior. Common law defines good or bad behavior by its effect on the rights of the individual or social institutions and doles out consequences for abridging these rights. If we say, for example, that the ends do or do not justify the means, we are applying philosophical principles that influence our understanding of meaning and truth. We have to know what the ends are and what the means are to judge a given moral act or choice. Moral or ethical decisions are also about consent, knowledge, freedom, motives, and the awareness of the consequences of moral acts or decisions. However, I don't think that it's possible to know, from a purely human philosophical point of view, what the best choice is and how to carry it out. Even our best intentions are limited by the choices of others, the social mores, our culture, and the human reality of our limited understanding. There is only one alternative to the quagmire of humanities, poverty, injustice, fragmented relationships, violence, and oppression. Yes, society can continue to chase its own tail of meaning with limited success. There are victories of science and culture, of education and business. Yet underneath these successes lies the shallow grave of mortality and meaning. There is only one person who has been raised above the limitation of our sin and hubris. He will not knock us down to control the outcome of our prospects for the future. He will raise us up to be with Him in the love of the Father in the Spirit.

Perhaps the deepest realization of the truth of our own mortality is when sickness comes upon us or when someone close to us dies. The inescapable reality of life's frailness washes over us; and now we know, through our grief, that we are going to face this thief ourselves. When end-of-life choices are presented to the person we love, they are also brought home to us. It's in these moments of darkness, when we can't see our way out, that the principles of Jesus we have discussed are most concentrated. He doesn't bring these pains and losses upon us to punish or hurt. They come all by themselves; they don't respect persons or ask for their permission. They come like a thief in the night, and when they come, we become aware of our emptiness.

I was going to Arizona State University when I was eighteen, and I had a late evening class. I got out after nine at night. I was walking to my old Chrysler in the parking lot. All the cars that had been there were gone. I had to walk quite a distance to get to it. My car was the only one left. It was parked under a solitary streetlight. When I got to it, I turned and looked all around. I suddenly became aware of my loneliness and isolation. The school that was so full of energy and life was vacant. It was a metaphor for all the things that I thought were so important. Someday they would all be gone. The sinking feeling of my vulnerability surrounded me. There, under that streetlight, in the darkness, I prayed that God would come into my life and bring meaning to it. There had been other times when I faced the darkness in my childhood because of my asthma; however, none of them stick out like this one. I think that my vocation began there. Perhaps that's why Jesus always took solitary time with His Father in the desert. He was in that dark place when He was arrested that night outside Jerusalem.

"He was a man well-acquainted with grief" (Is. 53:2–6). He was a man well aware of the human condition. Life is fleeting, just like human glory. The accolades of the crowd were still ringing in His ears. Yet there in the darkness, what He knew would come visited Him with a roar, like a lion, of pain and loss (Mark 14:32–41).

My dear wife, Dorothy, had been home several weeks from the hospital; and she was in good spirits working on some letters she wanted to send to our friends. She had recovered, but she was not well. With each hospitalization, Parkinson's had sapped more and more of her strength. When I walked into our apartment in Assisted Living that day, she was at her desk writing. She greeted me with her usual loving smile and said, matter-of-factually, "Michael, please don't take me back to the hospital." Her eyes returned to what she was doing, and then she looked back up at me and smiled. Nothing more needed to be said. We both knew that her decision was final, and that was what she wanted. I replied as tenderly as I could, "Okay, honey, you can stay here." She had faced the darkness and the roar of the lion. Now we had to live it out. The next day she took a turn for the worse, and forty-eight hours later, she met Jesus face-to-face.

It would be easy for me to return to that vacant darkness under the streetlight and stay there. Many people do; they ask, "Why did God do this to me?" They think that God is responsible for the darkness and the pain and loss of human sorrow. He must be to blame for our condition since He made us this way. Pain, loss, and sorrow can so easily turn to anger and resentment. We can become so fixated by loneliness that we don't see the streetlight over our head. We can turn to that light of Jesus. It shines in the darkness, and nothing can put it out. Dorothy knew about the light of God's love. She had experienced the love of Jesus since she was a little girl. The light had only grown in her heart over the years. We both faced the darkness with courage and with our calling.

The Glorious Gift of Faith Shines in the Darkness

St. John of the Cross talks about the "dark night of the soul." A lot of people think he is talking about depression or some psychological problem. St. Paul (2 Cor. 12:7) speaks about a condition that pained him and caused him to suffer. He comes to terms with it by saying that Christ's grace is sufficient, that when he is weak, then he is strong (2 Cor. 12: 7–10). His answer to the darkness is with faith, a belief that Jesus will see him through and that he is not alone. Faith is the antidote to the emptiness of the world's solutions. When there is a chronic illness, surgery, emotional brokenness, or relational breakups, the response of faith is the most powerful antidote.

I've been a chaplain for many years. It has been, and continues to be, an amazing experience to see the antidote of faith at work. I have seen miraculous recoveries, both because of medicine and sometimes in spite of it. Personal victories over infirmity, drug addiction, and other painful compulsions. They didn't happen without faith. They happened because of faith. With every moral, and ethical, choice comes the opportunity

to exercise faith. We place our trust in the doctor's treatment for our sickness. We believe the value of contracts and commerce. We accept the word of a friend or loved one. Society is dependent on faith, and trust, to bind it together. Without faith, there wouldn't, and couldn't, be any possibility for community. When our institutions are threatened because of fraud, selfishness, lies, and broken promises, then we are also in jeopardy of losing our freedoms. Without truthfulness, and faith, our human connections split apart; and we enter the darkness of self-protection, defensiveness, and moral hedonism.

Belief in God is not a huge leap. It's as normal as trusting a person we love and respect. It's a reasonable decision. If so much hinges on our human capacity to believe and trust one another, then the reality of faith in God initiates us into the deepest kind of societal bonding. We believe in someone, and then we can believe in something. We see this in the ministry of Jesus. He believes the Father, which leads Him to believe in His mission of redemption. Jesus opens the gates of the new creation, long since closed to us by Adam's sin, and leads the parade of God's people into that New Jerusalem (Rev. 22:1–5).

The most obvious and deepest connection to the new creation is our children. They are the promise and pledge of our divine inheritance. One of the many reasons they should be treated with love, dignity, and respect. They are so close in time to the new creation. When we love God, as Jesus does, then we will love ourselves and His people. Children are the most important expression of the new creation. We are privileged to care for them because they are a gift from God, an expression of His divine plan and purpose. They draw us into rediscovering the meaning of our own creation and purpose. They bring us in touch with the blessing of life and its potential. Children help to remind us of the reality of the new creation in ourselves and others. Jesus points this out to Nicodemus: "We must be born again" (John 3:1–21). The Holy Spirit conveys this gift of recovering what was lost by Adam's sin. Like Moses, (Exod. 34:29–35) the further we move along the timeline of maturity, this original glory fades, not just physically, but in other ways. Our innocence is easily lost with more and more experiences and by living in a culture that's in conflict with God's purposes. Often the culprit can be others who hurt or abuse a person. Sin passes on a legacy of lost innocence. The longer we live, the more we see the destructiveness of suffering, pain, and hardships. In a broken world, how can we recover lost innocence? "How can a man be born again?" Nicodemus asks Jesus, (Jn. 3:4) only the Holy Spirit makes this possible.

I have prayed for inner healing with many people who have suffered tremendous betrayals by those they should have been able to trust. Sometimes this is by physical or sexual abuse. How is it possible to move from fear, hurt, and alienation? Talking about it and counseling is very helpful, but how can we heal the past? God blesses our personal invitation, the Holy Spirit brings the new creation into the past hurts and suffering through grace and forgiveness. Innocence is recovered in the new creation through Jesus's grace of redemption in the Spirit. If we are a new creation in Christ, then what was lost is regained, "what was lost is found" (Luke 11:15–32). When Jesus is invited into a hurtful memory, forgiveness comes with the experience. It's quite mysterious how that happens. I never say things like "Now that we have prayed over that memory, you need to forgive the person who treated you so badly." No, quite the opposite. As Jesus heals the person's memory, at some point they will come to forgiveness on their own. It's as if the Spirit in that moment connects with the person's loss and pain and fabricates a new interior space of healing. The person becomes aware of their own need for God's grace and love, and with that comes the ability to forgive. The response to being emotionally and spiritually healed is forgiveness.

The Spirit alone can give the grace necessary to release a person from the bear hug of the past and at the same time open up the dark places in a person's soul. The light, through Jesus's incarnation and redemption, pours into the vacant broken heart; and innocence is reborn. The fruit of the new creation is planted, and the harvest of newness can be recovered and experienced.

The Language of the New Creation

It is amazing how children learn language. They make sounds that lead to words and from words laced with meaning to sentences and then to stories, translating sounds into a form of communication that is complex and ever changing. We work all our lives to broaden our vocabulary so that as we mature, we can share with others the experiences of life. Neurological connections lead to pathways that shape our understanding of the world and our place in it. Language is an essential part of knowing and becoming self-aware. It provides a framework for our history, relationships, and social/cultural interactions (Wagner & Hoff, 2012). We know who we are because we can communicate both verbally and non-verbally. God has a language too. It's a spiritual, internal connection to the new creation. The Holy Spirit communicates God's eternal love and acceptance through a spiritual language, similar to the one the apostles experienced in Pentecost (Acts 2:1–13). Praying in tongues does not mean that we have experienced all of the new creation. It means that we are now using God's language to listen and participate in the new creation. It may sound like baby talk, but every language starts the same way. Children mimic the sounds they hear; and soon those sounds, through repetitions, bloom into language. The Father places sounds in our hearts to speak a spiritual language to us. It connects us in the Holy Spirit to the universe of God's glory and our ministry of caring for one another. In Romans, Paul mentions the depth of God's Spirit in our spirit communicating the nature of our relationship with Him, in words that are groans of intimacy and longing (Rom. 8:14–17). After my wife died, I often would groan in the Spirit. I found praying in tongues a way of connecting with Jesus that was with words, not of my brain or consciousness, but out of my deepest pain and loss. No words could help me through the loss, and tears alone would not help. Praying in the Spirit connected me to the Lord in a way that my words could not contain. Often, I pray over a patient quietly in the Spirit. The doctors and nurses don't even know what is wrong with the patient. They often come into the hospital before all the tests are run to make a proper diagnosis. The Holy Spirit knows their need better than I do. Praying in the Spirit brings the prayer of Jesus to bear in the patient's situation and intercedes with the intention of the Holy Spirit for their well-being.

It's with virtue's paintbrush of glory that the Father's love in the Spirit colors everything. We can experience the depth of meaning in all things, even in suffering. The first chapter of this book started with the reality of human hardship. Through Christ's suffering, death, and resurrection, we can identify the process of the new creation. It's not just an outside ointment to soothe the conflict that plagues our world. The love of God is an interior movement in our soul, through God's grace, to meet the world and its brokenness with the victory of the resurrection and the caring of Jesus. If this is true, then the principles I have discussed in this book will inform our consciences to make good moral choices that conform to the relationship we have with Jesus. These principles are congruent with the nature of the Trinity. The love of Jesus impresses into our heart the capacity to "care for others as Christ cares for us." This "categorical imperative" follows the pattern of the life of Jesus, His teaching, His miracles, His prayer, and His communion with His Father. I have in this book tried not to settle moral questions with a system of philosophy or rules for human behavior. It's tempting to answer moral choices and decisions with laws and rules. We already have the common law and plenty of cultural mores for that kind of moral choice. Christianity is different. The person of Jesus is the center of the universe of making good choices. I have attempted in this book to raise the awareness of the principles that Jesus not only taught but lived.

Christians believe that Jesus is resurrected, and because He lives, we live in Him. The relationship we have with Jesus is the basis for appreciating the meaning of all our relationships. The principles and values that affirm healthy community, loving families, free individuals, and societies reside in the person of Jesus Christ. When Jesus says in John

14:6, "I am the way, the truth and the life," He is making an incarnational statement about Himself. This Scripture is a self-disclosure of who He is. We cannot say this about ourselves, because we cannot redeem and secure for ourselves eternal life. We are not in a position, because of human weakness and sin, to place ourselves in this context. Only in Jesus is there the new creation. He is the divine transcendence that draws us to the house of faith, that leads us to the doorway of hope, and that carries us across the threshold to God's home of love.

I have often observed a sign when properties are wanting to be sold by their owners: "Home for sale." How sad this advertisement is! A house can be sold, that's true; after all, it's a thing that can be replaced. A home is another matter—it's different. A home is greater than the sum of all the parts of a family. It should never be up for sale. A home is a spiritual thing; it's not real estate. It is the eternal estate of the bonding of relationships. Each person needs a home to take with them wherever they go. The memories, the friendships, the love and caring for each other live in our soul's home. It's an interior place, not a material thing at all. We may remember the place, but what we really know is who we are when we are at home. What our home stands for is its values, its meaning, its life. Since my wife died, I have thought about our home. I look over our pictures and remember what it was, and is, to be at home. I live in a nice one-bedroom apartment. It's a pleasant living arrangement. My home is there because I'm there. My life, my way of living, is inside my heart. My memories and dreams are in my home. We carry this with us always, and we know it, because Jesus is in the center of it all. We are not homeless when we are loved and when we love others. We are not homeless because we have the Word and the sacraments. We are never homeless because the Father has made His home in us through Jesus. When people believe that they are homeless, every kind of misbehavior and evil is possible. It's like the television show entitled *The Living Dead*. So many people today have lost their sense of being at home. Drug addiction tries to medicate the suffering of grief and physical and emotional pain. It leaves behind anger and resentment, which leads to violence by taking revenge for our home's absence. Divorce and broken relationships pressurize pain and failure, and our personal world shrinks down to meaninglessness and folly.

Jesus will make His home with us. He will wait on us at the table and feed us His body and blood. He does this so that we may live at home with Him. It's His incarnational pledge to us. We may be without a house, but we are never homeless. Even now, the Holy Spirit is preparing a place with us to be at home with God forever. We are no longer living for ourselves but for Him (Eph. 3:14–20). The Lord of perfect communion is also the Lord of loving and free choices.

It's obvious that one choice leads to another and then to another. There are only two options: choices that lead us closer to God or choices that move us further away from Him. Those that conform to the heart of Jesus move us into an ever-deepening relationship with God and build an ever-deepening sense of belonging. Choices that are selfish, proud, and arrogant chip away at our sense of belonging and being at home with God. We may live in a beautiful house, with the finest clothes and cars; but there is no home without love, respect, and caring. I have counseled many couples over my forty years of ministry. Husbands and wives may be married, but often they are not at home with each other. Often the very love, and caring, that they need to give each other they withhold. The interesting thing about this absence of bonding, of belonging, and of mutuality is both parties so desperately need and want to be at home. When it's absent, then resentment and anger produce fear and isolation (Hendrix, 1988).

Longing for Our Perfect Home

I believe that we know something about what our perfect home is and what it looks like. I don't mean about the furniture or design or shape, but we are seeking a connection to God's perfect home. It's a notion that is deeply embedded in our psyche. That seed was planted in the Garden of Eden long ago. We still carry the good earth of the new creation with us today. We hope that others will fit into this pattern, somehow expecting them to fill the desire for our homeland. It's often easier to expect others to do what we are called to be. Being at home in the new creation is not for someone else, but for each one of us. Living in the principles of Jesus brings the new creation home in our hearts.

Moral choices are personal choices. They reveal the nature of our beliefs, the nature of the bonding we have in our relationship to God and our neighbor.

Someday, when Jesus comes back again, the blessing of our liberation will be revealed for everyone to see. The vision that we have held on to will be an event of eternal glory. One thing is certain, we will be like Him (2 Cor. 5:1–6). We will be fully clothed in the Holy Spirit and wrapped up in timeless exaltation, a "new creation."

Finis

References

American Family Association, https://afajournal.org

Bonhoeffer, D., (1937, 1995 ed.). *Cost of Discipleship,* New York, N.Y., Touchstone

DeGrazia, D., Mappes, T. A., Brand-Ballard, J., (2011, 7th ed.). *Biomedical Ethics,* New York, N.Y. McGraw Hill Co.

Book of Common Prayer, (1979 ed.), New York, N.Y., Oxford University Press.

Brown, R. E., Fitzmyer, J., Murphy, R. E., (1968). *Jerome Biblical Commentary.* New York, N.Y., Pearson Publishers

CDC Centers for Disease Control and Prevention, (2018). https://nwucdc.gov/nchsdata/national-marriage-divorce-rates-00-18pdf

Computers and their impact, (retrieved 2020) www.csun.edu/lic42878/computers.html/calstateuniversitynorthridge.

Cursillo.org. A Cursillo, is a short course in Christianity with a three day retreat and an apostolic movement founded in 1944 in Spain.

Galton, F., (1921). *Eugenics* is a set of beliefs and practices to improve the genetic quality of a human population by excluding people or groups deemed as inferior. New questions have arisen because of new assisted reproduction technology, gestational surrogacy, pre-implantation, genetic diagnosis, cytoplasmic transfer.

Gallup Poll, (2018). https//news.gallup.com/poll/248837/church-membership-down-sharply-past-two-decades.aspx

Garrigou-Lagrange, R., (1989 ed.). *The Three Ages of the Interior Life,* Charlotte, N.C., Tan Books

Good News for Modern Man Bible, (2001, 2nd ed.). Grand Rapids, Ml. Zondervan Scripture used for all quotes and biblical quotations.

Hendrix, H., (1988). *Getting the Love you Want,* New York, N.Y., Henry Holt Co.

Ignatius of Loyola, (1914, ed.). *The Spiritual Exercises of St. Ignatius of Loyola,* New York, N.Y., Kennedy and Sons.

ISRA, (2018). *Risk Factors for Youth Violence; Youth Violence Commission,* (International Society on Aggression), Doi:10.1002/ab.21766

Jesus Seminar, (1985). is the work of 50 scholars who agreed that probably 20% of the quotes attributed to Jesus come directly from the source (see Westar Institute)

John of the Cross, (1991, ed.). *Living Flame of Love,* Washington, D.C. ICS Publications

John Paul II, (1995). *Evangalium Vitae,* http://www.papalencyclicals.net

Kant, I., (1999 ed.). *Critique of Pure Reason,* Cambridge, U.K., Cambridge University Press.

Law and Order, (first aired, 1990). creator Dick Wolf, NBC

Lessard, M., (2017). *Christology of the Family,* Enumclaw, Washington, Redemption Press

Maier, S. F., Seligman, M. E. P., (2016). Learned helplessness at fifty: Insights from neuroscience, *American Psychological Association,* https//Doi.org/10.1037

Marx, K., Engels, F., (1969 ed.). *Selected Works,* Vol. 1, Moscow, Russia, Progress Publishing

Maher, B., *Real time with Bill Maher,* https://www.hbo.com/real-time-with-bill-maher

McLuhan, M., (1967). *The Media is the Message,* Rutherford, N.J., Penguin Books

Metz, J. B., (1968, 1998). *Poverty of Spirit,* New York, N.Y. The Missionary Society of Saint Paul the Apostle

Minarik, J. D., (2017). Privilege as psychology: Making the dynamic and complex nature of privilege and marginalization accessible, *Journal of Social Work Educators,* 53(1)

Moyers, B., *Moyers Journal,* https://www.pbs.org/moyers/journal/index.html

Nguyen, C., (1993). A linkage between DNA markers on the x chromosome and male sexual orientation Hamer, D. H & Thomas, C. A., *Embryo Project Encyclopedia,* http://embryo.asu.edu/handle/10776/11476

NIH, National Institute of Health, https://www.nih.gov

NRLC, National Right to Life, www.nrlc.org statistics from (1973 to 20)

Peck, S. M., (1978, 1999). *A Road Less Traveled,* New York, N.Y. Simon & Shuster

Organista, P. B., Marin, G., Chun, K., (2018, 2nd ed.). *Psychology in a Multicultural World,* Los Angeles, Sage Publications

Pew Research Center, (2019). In the US decline of Christianity continues at a rapid rate, https://wwwpewforum.org/2019/1017/in-us-decline-of-christianity-continues-at-a-rapid-rate.

Savage, J. *Listening & Caring Skills, A Guide for Groups and Leaders,* Nashville, TN., Abingdon Press

Hesman, T. S., (2019). No evidence that gay gene exists, *Science,* news.org/noevidence-that-gay-gene-exists

Tillich, P., (1957, 1975). *Systematic Theology. Volume 2,* Chicago, Il., Chicago University Press

Tournier, P., (1962). *Guilt and Grace,* New York, N.Y., Harper and Row

Von Balthazar, Hans Urs, (1967). *Theological Anthropology,* New York, N.Y., Sheed and Ward

Walking Dead, created by, Kirkman, R., Moore, T., Adlard, C., (2010). Fox Broadcasting Co., www.amc.com.

Wagner, L., Hoff, E., (2019). *Handbook of Psychology,* Hoboken, N.J., John Wiley and Sons.

www.ingramcontent.com/pod-product-compliance
Lightning Source LLC
Chambersburg PA
CBHW060358080526
44583CB00012B/369